HINDOO STORIES

Collected and Collated by
ANARYAN

Smriti Books

ISBN: 81-87967-02-1

Indian Edition: 2000
Reprint: 2001

First Edition: 1881

Publishers
SMRITI BOOKS
(an imprint of)
SPB Enterprises
124, Siddhartha Enclave
New Delhi-110 014 (INDIA)
Email: sunitapb@hotmail.com
Website: www.spbenterprises.com

Distributors
NEW AGE BOOKS
A-44 Naraina Phase I
New Delhi-110 028 (INDIA)
Email: info@newagebooksindia.com
Website: www.newagebooksindia.com

Printed in India
by Jainendra Prakash Jain at Shri Jainendra Press
A-45 Naraina Phase-I New Delhi-110 028

INDEX OF CONTENTS.

CHAPTER VI.

CHAPTER VII.

CHAPTER VIII.

CHAPTER IX.

PREFACE.

Competent authorities assert that the conversation of mankind at the earliest stage of their existence was monosyllabic; men and women addressed each other in words of a single syllable, now considered as the roots or basis of our present languages. It is presumed that after humanity got over the root stage, and well into the syllabic epoch, they began to tell each other stories, and these being constantly repeated, were handed down to posterity *vivâ voce*. As time went on the art of writing became known, consisting at first of single figures representing what was intended to be expressed; for as the root was the first stage of language, so the single figure was the first stage of writing. After a further period, alphabets were introduced, and the early figures and representations were changed into words composed of letters. And then the fables or stories, which had been going the rounds so long from mouth to mouth, were gradually put into writing, and after centuries and centuries eventually found themselves in print. As the East was far in advance of the West in civilization, it is probable that the former was the cradle of many tales; and that stories, told first there in original, have filtered through many countries and many channels till they were served up again in the West, sometimes with additions and sometimes without.

The short fable may, then, be considered as the first means of imparting instruction and amusement to man. As years rolled by the fable grew into the tale or story, which later on expanded into the romance and the novel. The fable deals chiefly with men, women, animals, birds, insects, and fish, they being the active parts of their ingredients; description of things, times, and places being the passive. Each fable is designed to illustrate and exemplify some precept for human conduct, and what is said by the animal, bird, insect, or fish applies more to men and women than to themselves.

Among the mass of fable, tale, or story, it is difficult to select specimens to suit the tastes of all. Excessive wit is as rare as excessive beauty, and it cannot be expected that all the stories are gems. While a few are good, some fair, and many indifferent, all are interesting as giving the thoughts, the ideas, the sentiments, and the actions of the humanities from the earliest ages. Generally they may be divided into four groups—viz., the Sanscrit or Hindoo group, the Arabic and Persian group, the Western or European group, and the American group. Of these the Sanscrit stories are the oldest, and probably served as the basis of the Arabic and Persian tales, which again can be traced as the source from which many of the European authors took their start. American wit and humour, as exemplified in their tales and sketches, form a group of themselves, and seem to have originated in the land which is itself the latest novelty, and which, at present, has the greatest future before it. While much of the European facetiousness can be traced to an Eastern origin, the American ideas stand out by themselves the product of a civilization which has, in a certain way, civilized itself, and produced much original matter. The different groups will, however, be dealt with separately, and the present volume contains only specimens of Hindoo tales and stories.

With the exception of some stories which are now translated for the first time, this book contains nothing new. Much has been borrowed from the works of Sir William Jones, H. T. Colebrooke, and H. H. Wilson, the early pioneers and investigators of Sanscrit literature, and who laid the foundations of the edifice, which has been added to largely by the learned professors Max Muller, Monier Williams, Francis Johnson, George Bühler, and others. I am also indebted to Mr. P. W. Jacob for extracts from his translation of the adventures of the ten princes, a story as interesting as the Arabian nights, and giving illustrations of the Hindoo character both in idea and action. The same may be said of the adventures of Vickramaditya, king of Oojein, translated into English by Ragoba Moraba, of Bombay; and of the stories of the thirty-two statues, partly translated by Sayud Abdullah. Other authors and translators, from whose works much has been taken, have all been duly acknowledged in some part of the present collection.

INTRODUCTION.

Before commencing an analysis of certain Hindoo story-books, it is advisable to give a few details of the domestic and social life of the Hindoos themselves, as described by the learned sage, Vatsyayana, who wrote about the beginning of the Christian era. The exact date of his work is unknown, but from the use of certain words, and from allusions to other writings and other persons, it is supposed to have been written not earlier than the first, and not later than the third century, A.D.

The work itself is well known in Sanscrit literature as the Vatsyayana Kama Sutra, or Aphorisms on Love by Vatsyayana, and is the standard work on love, and social and domestic life in that language. It was composed by Vatsya, while leading the life of a religious student at Benares; at all events that is what he himself says at the close of the manuscript. It further appears that he had carefully studied the writings of seven earlier authors, whose names he mentions, but none of whose works are now extant. In other literature of the same nature, but of a later date, Vatsyayana is always quoted as the chief authority on these subjects.

The work is interesting on account of its undoubted age and genuineness. It contains, however, a good deal of matter connected with the domestic and private details of married life to which it is unnecessary to allude, and which are more fitted for Sanscrit manuscript than for English print. But the remarks on the subjects of education, on the study of the sixty-four arts, on the kind of life to be led by a householder, his household arrangements, his friends and companions, his occupations and amusements, his conduct to the fair sex, and his marriage, are simple and good. They show that the Hindoos of that age possessed a civilization far in advance of our own at that time, while the exact details of everything to be done by husbands and wives seem to point out that marriage obligations were fully recognized at that period.

From the earliest ages down to the present time the Hindoos have based their ideas of life on three things—viz., Dharma, Artha, and Kama, three words constantly found in their literature.

"Dharma" may be translated as the acquisition of virtue or religious merit, and obedience to the ordinances of religion. It is to be learnt from the holy writ, and from those conversant with it. In a word, it is "Religion," the basis of all good.

"Artha" may be translated as the acquisition of arts, land, gold, cattle, wealth, equipages and friends. It is further the protection of what is acquired, and the increase of what is protected, or, in other words, keeping what we have got, and acquiring more. It is to be learnt from the king's officers, and from merchants who may be well acquainted with the ways of commerce.

"Kama" is the enjoyment of appropriate objects by the five senses of hearing, feeling, seeing, tasting, and smelling, assisted by the mind, together with the soul. The ingredient in this is a peculiar contact between the organ of sense and its object, and the consciousness of pleasure which arises from that contact is called Kama. It is to be learnt from the aphorisms on the senses, and from the practice of citizens.

Keeping the above three things constantly in view, the rules about education, and the study of the arts and sciences, are then laid down. Parents are enjoined to indulge their children until they attain the age of five; from five to sixteen they are to be instructed in the fourteen sciences and the sixty-four arts, or some of them; and after sixteen they are only to be verbally admonished.

The fourteen sciences include the study of the Vedas, the Poorans and Oopupoorans, the Dhurmsastru, law, medicine, music, military and mechanical sciences, astronomy and astrology, arithmetic, grammar, pronunciation, cosmography, physics, and metaphysics.

A complete list of the sixty-four arts has been given by Vatsyayana, and are quoted here to show the state of civilization of the Hindoos at that early period. They are as follow:—

1. Singing.
2. Playing on musical instruments.
3. Dancing.
4. Union of dancing, singing, and playing instrumental music.
5. Writing and drawing.
6. Tattooing.
7. Arraying and adorning an idol with rice and flowers.
8. Spreading and arranging beds or couches of flowers, or flowers upon the ground.
9. Colouring the teeth, garments, hair, nails, and bodies—*i.e.*, staining, dyeing, colouring, and painting the same.
10. Fixing stained glass into a floor.
11. The art of making beds, and spreading out carpets and cushions for reclining.
12. Playing on musical glasses filled with water.
13. Storing and accumulating water in aqueducts, cisterns, and reservoirs.
14. Picture making, limning, and decorating.
15. Stringing of rosaries, necklaces, garlands, and wreaths.
16. Binding of turbans and chaplets, and making crests and top-knots of flowers.
17. Scenic representations. Stage playing.
18. Art of making ear ornaments.
19. Art of preparing perfumes and odours.
20. Proper disposition of jewels and decorations, and adornment in dress.
21. Magic or sorcery.
22. Quickness of hand, or manual skill.

23. Culinary art—*i.e.*, cooking and cookery.
24. Making lemonades, sherbets, acidulated drinks, and spirituous extracts, with proper flavour and colour.
25. Tailors' work and sewing.
26. Making parrots, flowers, tufts, tassels, bunches, bosses, knobs, &c., out of yarn or thread.
27. Solution of riddles, enigmas, covert speeches, verbal puzzles, and enigmatical questions.
28. A game which consisted in repeating verses, and as one person finished, another person had to commence at once, repeating another verse, beginning with the same letter with which the last speaker's verse ended. Whoever failed to repeat was considered to have lost, and to be subject to pay a forfeit or stake of some kind.
29. The art of mimicry or imitation.
30. Reading, including chanting and intoning.
31. Study of sentences difficult to pronounce. It is played as a game chiefly by women and children, and consists of a difficult sentence being given, and when repeated quickly, the words are often transposed or badly pronounced.
32. Practice with sword, single stick, quarter staff, and bow and arrow.
33. Drawing inferences, reasoning or inferring.
34. Carpentry, or the work of a carpenter.
35. Architecture, or the art of building.
36. Knowledge about gold and silver coins, and jewels and gems.

37. Chemistry and mineralogy.
38. Colouring jewels, gems, and beads.
39. Knowledge of mines and quarries.
40. Gardening, knowledge of treating the diseases of trees and plants, of nourishing them, and determining their ages.
41. Art of cock fighting, quail fighting, and ram fighting.
42. Art of teaching parrots and starlings to speak.
43. Art of applying perfumed ointments to the body, and of dressing the hair with unguents and perfumes, and braiding it.
44. The art of understanding writing in cypher, and the writing of words in a peculiar way. Also the art of understanding the signs made by the fingers, each sign having an alphabetical meaning.
45. The art of speaking by changing the forms of words. It is of various kinds. Some speak by changing the beginning and end of words, others by adding unnecessary letters between every syllable of a word, and so on.
46. Knowledge of languages, and of the vernacular dialects.
47. Art of making flower earriages.
48. Art of framing mystical diagrams, of addressing spells and charms, and binding armlets.
49. Mental exercises, such as completing stanzas or verses on receiving a part of them; or

supplying one, two, or three lines when the remaining lines are given indiscriminately from different verses, so as to make the whole an entire verse with regard to its meaning; or arranging the words of a verse written irregularly, by separating the vowels from the consonants, or leaving them out altogether; or putting into verse or prose sentences represented by signs or symbols. There are many other such exercises.

50. Composing poems.
51. Knowledge of dictionaries and vocabularies.
52. Knowledge of ways of changing and disguising the appearance of persons.
53. Knowledge of the art of changing the appearance of things, such as making cotton to appear as silk, coarse and common things to appear as fine and good.
54. Various ways of gambling.
55. Art of obtaining possession of the property of others by means of Muntras or incantations.
56. Skill in youthful sports.
57. Knowledge of the rules of society, and of how to pay respects and compliments to others.
58. Knowledge of the art of war, of arms, armies, &c.
59. Knowledge of gymnastics.
60. Art of knowing the character of a man from his features.

61. Knowledge of scanning or constructing verses.
62. Arithmetical recreations.
63. Making artificial flowers.
64. Making figures and images in clay.

After remarks on education, details are then given about the life of a citizen, the translation of which runs thus:

Having thus been educated, a man should become a householder, with the wealth that he may have gained by gift, conquest, purchase, deposit, or by inheritance from his ancestors. He should take a house in a city, or in a large village, or in the vicinity of good men, or in the neighbourhood of his friends. This abode should be situated near good water, and should be divided into different compartments for various purposes. It should be surrounded by a garden, and should also contain two rooms—an outer and an inner room. The inner room should be occupied by the females of the family; while the outer room, balmy with rich perfumes, should contain a bed—soft, agreeable to the sight, covered with a clean white cloth, low in the middle part, having garlands and bunches of flowers upon it, and a canopy above, and two pillows, one at the top and another at the bottom. There should be also a couch besides, and at the head of this a stool, on which should be placed fragrant ointments for the night, as well as flowers, pots containing collyrium and other fragrant substances; things used for perfuming the mouth, and the bark of the common citron tree. Near the bed, on the ground, there should be a pot for spitting after eating betel leaves, a box for jewels and ornaments, a lute hanging from a peg made of the tusk of an elephant, a board for drawing, and some garlands of the yellow amaranth. Not far from the bed, again on the ground, there should be a round seat, a toy cart, and a board for playing with dice. Outside the outer room there should be cages of birds, and also a separate room for spinning, carving, and such like diversions. In the garden there should be a whirling swing and a common swing, also a bower of creepers covered with flowers, in which a raised parterre should be made for sitting on.

Now, the householder having got up in the morning, and performed his necessary duties, should then wash his teeth, apply a limited quantity of ointments and perfumes to his body, put some ornaments on his person, and collyrium on his eyelids and below his eyes, colour his lips with alaktaka, and look at himself in the glass. Then having eaten betel leaves with other things that give fragrance to the mouth, he should then perform his usual business. He should bathe daily, anoint his body with oil every other day, apply a lathering substance to his body every three days, get his head shaved every four days, and his body every ten days. All these things should be done without fail. Meals should be taken in the forenoon, the afternoon, and again at night. After the morning meal, parrots and other birds should be taught to speak, and the fighting of cocks, quails, and rams should follow. A limited time should be devoted to seeing his friends and confidants, parasites and jesters; and then should follow the noon-day repose. In the afternoon, having put on his clothes and his ornaments, the householder should converse with his friends. In the evening there should be singing and social amusements.

The following are the things to be done occasionally as diversions or amusements, viz.:—

1. Holding festivals in honour of different deities.
2. Social gatherings of both sexes.
3. Drinking parties.
4. Picnics.
5. Other social diversions,

Details of which are given, along with a description of the companions and friends, and messengers of the imaginary citizen. The qualities of friends are that—

They should tell the truth.

They should not be changed by time.

They should be favourable to your designs.

They should be firm.

They should be free from covetousness.

They should not be capable of being gained over by others.

They should not reveal your secrets.

And the kind of friends that should be attached to any person are—

One who played with you in the dust—*i.e.*, in childhood.

One who is bound by an obligation.

One who is of the same disposition, and fond of the same things.

One who is a fellow student.

One who is acquainted with your secrets and faults, and whose faults and secrets are also known to you.

One who is a child of your nurse.

One who is brought up with you.

One who is an hereditary friend.

And as regards messengers, the qualities required of them are—

Skilfulness.

Boldness.

Knowledge of the intention of men and of their outward signs.

Absence of confusion—*i.e.*, no shyness.

Knowledge of the exact meaning of what others do or say.

Good manners.

Knowledge of appropriate times and places for doing different things.

Ingenuity in business.

Quick comprehension.

Quick application of remedies—*i. e.*, quick and ready resources.

And the chapter ends with a verse to the effect that the man who is ingenuous and wise, who is accompanied by a friend, and who judges well the intentions of others, and who knows the proper time and place for doing everything, generally accomplishes his purpose, and succeeds tolerably well in this world in all his undertakings.

Long details are then given about marriage and the acquisition of a wife, how to make love to a fair maiden, and how to win her; plenty of conversation being one of the necessities, for, says the sage, "Though a man loves a girl ever so much, he never succeeds in winning her without a great deal of talking." The parents of the girl also have to do their share. It is laid down that when a girl becomes marriageable, her parents should dress her smartly and place her where she can be easily seen by all. Every afternoon, having dressed her and decorated her in a becoming manner, they should send her with female companions to sports, sacrifices, and marriage ceremonies, and thus show her to advantage, because she is a kind of merchandise. The parents should also receive with kind words and signs of friendliness those of an auspicious appearance and character, who may come accompanied by their friends and relations for the purpose of marrying their daughter. What the parents are to do, what the man is to do, and what the girl is to do, are all given with that detail and classification which the Hindoos dearly love, but too lengthy to be repeated here. Passing over these, we then come to the duties of a wife, which are described as follows:—

A virtuous woman, who has affection for her husband, should act in conformity with his wishes as if he was a divine being, and, with his consent, should take upon herself the whole care of his family. She should keep the house well cleaned, and arrange flowers of various kinds in different parts of it, and make the floor smooth and polished, so as to give the whole a nice and becoming appearance. She should place ready in it all the materials required for the morning, noon, and evening sacrifices, and she should herself revere the sanctuary of the household gods, for, says Gonardiya, "Nothing so much attracts the heart of a householder to his wife as a careful observance of the things mentioned above." Towards the parents, relations, friends, servants, and sisters of her husband, she should behave as they deserve. In the garden she should plant beds of green vegetables, bunches of the sugar cane, and clumps of the fig-tree, the mustard plant, the parsley plant, the fennel plant, and the xanthochymus pictorius; clusters of various flowers, such as the trapa bispinosa, the jasmine, the gasminum grandiflorum, the yellow amaranth, the wild jasmine, the tabernæmontana coronaria, the china rose, and others, should likewise be planted, together with the fragrant grass andropogon schœnanthus, and the fragrant root of the plant andropogon miricatus. She should also have seats and arbours made in the garden, in the middle of which a well, tank, or pool should be dug. She should always avoid the company of female beggars, female Buddhist mendicants, unchaste and roguish women, female fortune-tellers and witches. As regards meals, she should always consider what her husband likes and dislikes, and what things are good for him, and what are injurious to him. When she hears the sound of his footsteps coming home, she should at once get up and be ready to do whatever he may command her, and either order her female servant to wash his feet or wash them herself. When going anywhere with her husband she should put on her ornaments, and should not give or accept invitations, or attend marriages and sacrifices, or sit in the company of female friends, or visit the temple of the gods without his consent. If she wishes to engage in any kinds of games or sports, she should not do it against his will. In the same way she should always sit down after him and get up before him, and should never awaken him when he is asleep. The kitchen should be situated in a quiet and retired place, so as not to be accessible to strangers, and it should always look nice. In the event of any misconduct on the part of her husband, she should not blame him excessively, even though she be a little displeased. She should not use abusive language towards him, but rebuke him with conciliatory words, whether he be in the company of friends or alone. She should not also be a scold, for, says Gonardya, "There is no cause of dislike on the part of the husband so great as this characteristic in his wife." Lastly, she should avoid bad expressions, bad looks, speaking aside, standing in the doorway and looking at passers by; conversing in pleasure groves, and remaining in a lonely place for a long time; and, finally, she should always keep her body, her teeth, her hair, and everything belonging to her nice, sweet, and clean."

When the wife wants to go to her husband in private, her dress should consist of many ornaments, various kinds of flowers, a cloth decorated with different colours, and some sweet-smelling ointments or unguents. Her every-day dress should be made up of a thin close-textured cloth, a few ornaments and flowers, and a little scent—not too much. She should also observe the fasts and vows of her husband, and when he tries to prevent her doing this, she should persuade him to let her do it.

At appropriate times of the year, and when they happen to be cheap, she should buy earth, bamboos, firewood, skins, and iron pots, as also salt and oil. Fragrant substances, vessels made of the fruit of the plant wrightea antidysenterica, or oval-leaved wrightea, medicines, and other things which are always wanted, should be obtained when required, and kept in a secret place of the house. The seeds of the radish, the potato, the common beet, the damanaka (Indian wormwood), the mangoe, the cucumber, the egg plant, the kushmanda, the pumpkin gourd, the surana, the bignonia indica, the sandal wood, the premna spinosa, the garlic plant, onions, and other plants should be bought and sown at the proper seasons.

The wife, moreover, should not tell to strangers the amount of her wealth, nor the secrets which her husband has confided to her. She should surpass all the women of her own rank in life in her cleverness, her appearance, her knowledge of cookery, her pride, and her manner of serving her husband. The expenditure of the year should be regulated by the profits; and the milk that remains, after being used at meals, should be turned into ghee or clarified butter. Oil and sugar should be prepared at home; spinning and weaving should also be done there; and a store of ropes and cords, and barks of trees for twisting into ropes, should be kept. She should also attend to the pounding and cleaning of rice, using its small grain and chaff in some way or other. She should pay the salaries of the servants, look after the tilling of the fields, the keeping of the flocks and herds, superintend the making of vehicles, and take care of the rams, cocks, quails, parrots, starlings, cuckoos, peacocks, monkeys, and deer; and finally, adjust the income and expenditure of the day. The worn-out clothes should be given to those servants who have done good work, in order to show them that their services have been appreciated, or they may be applied to some other use. The vessels in which wine is prepared, as well as those in which it is kept, should be carefully looked after, and used at the proper time. All sales and purchases should also be well attended to.

The friends of her husband she should welcome by presenting them with flowers, ointment, incense, betel leaves, and betel nut. Her father-in-law and mother-in-law she should treat as they deserve, always remaining dependent on their will; never contradicting them; speaking to them in few and not harsh words; not laughing loudly in their presence, and acting with their friends and enemies as with her own. In addition to the above, she should not be vain, or too much taken up with her enjoyments; should be liberal towards her servants, and reward them on holidays and festivals, and should not give anything to any body without first making it known to her husband.

During the absence of her husband on a journey, the wife should wear only her auspicious ornaments, and observe the fasts in honour of the gods. While anxious to hear the news of her husband, she should still look after her household affairs. She should sleep near the elder women of the house, and make herself agreeable to them. She should look after and keep in repair the things that are liked by her husband, and the works that have been begun by him should be continued. To the houses of her relations she should not go, except on occasions of joy and sorrow, and then she should go in the usual travelling dress, accompanied by her husband's servants, and should not remain there for a long time. The fasts and feasts should be observed with the consent of the elders of the house. The resources should be increased by making purchases and sales according to the practice of merchants, and by means of honest servants superintended by herself. The income should be increased, and the expenditure diminished as much as possible. And when her husband returns from his journey, she should receive him in her ordinary clothes, so that he may know in what way she has lived during his absence, and should bring to him some presents, as also materials for the worship of the deity.

And the chapter concludes with the following verse:—

"The wife, whether she be a woman of noble

ıamily, or a virgin widow remarried, or a concubine, should lead a chaste life, devoted to her husband, and doing everything for his welfare. Thus they acquire Dharma, Artha, and Kama, occupy a high position, and keep their husbands devoted to them."

Details are then given concerning the conduct of the elder wife towards the other wives of her husband, and the conduct of the younger wife towards the elder ones. Also on the conduct of a virgin widow remarried, of a wife disliked by her husband, and of the women in the king's harem, and lastly on the conduct of a husband towards many wives.

Other chapters then follow, entering into great details about marriages, about the wives of other people, and about courtesans. To persons unacquainted with the social domestic economy of the Hindoos, the subtle analysis of their feelings on these subjects would require to be more fully explained than by the few cursory lines which are all that could be given in this present volume. The matter is all there, but a Balzac is required to place it in an interesting way before the public. The introduction, already long, must be brought now to a close.

A GROUP
OF
HINDOO STORIES.

CHAPTER I.

Of the Fables of Bidpai or Pilpai, and the Pancha Tantra.

The oldest collection of tales are those traditionally known as the fables of Bidpai, or Pilpai. The author of them is unknown, as also the date of their production, and no edition of them is in existence. A good deal has been written about them both by Jones and Wilson, De Sacy, and Deslongchamps, but in the absence of any manuscript, or tangible proof, their writings can only be founded on ideas and conjectures. Tradition, however, says that they were written in Sanscrit, that they were the earliest work of the kind, and that they have been reproduced in the Pancha Tantra, or five chapters, or five sections, and in the Hitopodesa, or Friendly Advice.

The Pancha Tantra is so called from its being divided into five Tantras, or chapters, but it is better known to the public by the name of the Panchopákhyána, or the five collection of stories, and under this name it is common in India.

Its date cannot be fixed, but the author is supposed to be one Vishnu Sarma, and it was written for the education of the king's sons in prose, and divided into five chapters.

I. Dissension of friends.
II. Acquisition of friends.
III. Inveterate enmity.
IV. Loss of advantage.
V. Inconsiderateness.

The story opens that there was once a king who had three sons, all wanting in diligence and intelligence. Having consulted his counsellors, they advised that the education of his sons should be entrusted to a learned Brahman, named Vishnu Sarma, who accordingly takes them in hand, and the result of what he teaches them, or rather his lessons, are embodied in the book. As the princes became highly accomplished in six months, the Pancha Tantra naturally became famous throughout the world.

The book is full of stories, and aphorisms, and descriptions of how to conduct yourself under various circumstances of life. The greater part of the stories relate to animals, what they do, and how they act, when in danger or difficulty, in prosperity or adversity. The first chapter contains thirty-one stories, the second eight, the third seventeen, the fourth twelve, and the fifth twelve; but these vary in different editions, and the exact number cannot be definitely fixed. The following will, however, serve as specimens of the whole:—

Excessive cupidity is to be avoided, though all desire of profit need not be relinquished. The wheel whirls round his head, who evinced inordinate avarice, as the following story shows:—

In a certain town there dwelt four Brahmans, all intimate friends and equally poor. They consulted together what was to be done, for poverty, they agreed, was intolerable. Patrons, however well attended, are dissatisfied; friends and sons desert the poor; merit is of no avail, and misfortunes multiply. Wives of the best families abandon their husbands; friends transfer their attachment to more powerful individuals. Again, let a man be brave, handsome, eloquent, and learned, without wealth, he does not obtain any enjoyment, and is as a dead man among the living. Better death than poverty. Again it is said, "Arise, my friend, for a moment, and remove the burden of indigence from my fate, that I may share with you the felicity which death affords. It is better, therefore, to go to the cemetery at once, and become a corpse than to live in poverty." The friends assented to this, and agreed that every effort should be adopted to acquire wealth, as it is said, "Nothing is obtained by him who has not money. Let, therefore, the wise man attach himself to its acquirement." Wealth is acquirable by six means—viz., begging, service, agriculture, science, usury, and trade, of which trade is the best, as its profits are most independently realized. As it has been observed: the food obtained as alms may be carried off by crows; the favour of a prince or patron may be withdrawn; agriculture is laborious; and the respect to be paid to a preceptor in acquiring knowledge is troublesome; usury brings poverty on other people, so that the only method eligible is trade. Money is made in trade in seven ways: by defective weights and measures; by false statements of price; by the lapse of deposits; by receiving the securities of friends; by managing the estates of others; by dealing in perfumes; and by exporting goods for sale. In the first case it is pretended that the measure is full, when it is not. In the second, selling a thing for more than its worth is the natural practice even of barbarians. While a deposit is in his house the merchant prays to the gods that the owner may die, when he will make them suitable offerings. When a trader sees an acquaintance coming to borrow, he pretends to lament his misfortune, but is inwardly delighted. In the management of estates there is always the reflection that I have got hold of lands full of treasure. Of all goods perfumes are the best: gold is not to be compared to the article which is procured for one piece, and is parted with for a thousand pieces. Exporting commodities is the proper business of persons already wealthy, as it is said, "Those who are wealthy are heard of from afar. Riches are attracted by riches, as wild elephants are caught by tame ones." Capital is multiplied twice and thrice over in repeatedly buying and selling by those who have knowledge, and who travel to other lands. The idle and the weak alone are afraid of foreign countries. Crows, deer, and dastards die in their native place.

Having thus reflected, the four friends determined to quit their homes, and to set off together to travel. The man whose mind is intent on wealth leaves his friends and his family, his mother and his natal soil, and roams to foreign and ungenial lands without a moment's hesitation. After some days the Brahmans arrived at Avanti, where they bathed in the Sipra and worshipped Mahákala; after which they proceeded on their way, and met a Yogi named Bhairavanada, with whom they formed an acquaintance, and who invited them to his abode. He inquired of them the purpose of their journey. They said, "We are pilgrims in search of magic power, repairing to the shrine where wealth or death awaits us, as it is said, 'The water that falls from Heaven may sometimes flow in the realms below the earth. The force of fate is inconceivable, and man is weak against it. The objects of man may be apparently attained by mortal efficacy; but that is fate: for when you speak of human qualities you give that name to destiny. At the same time ease is not here the source of ease, nor can it be enjoyed without exertion. The destroyer of Madhu seized Lakshmi forcibly and held her clasped in a firm embrace.' Tell us therefore," they continued, "if you are acquainted with any drug of virtue to carry us into secret chasms, and tame the imps of evil; or do you know any thing efficacious in the rites of charnel grounds? You are an adept, we are only novices, but we are resolute. None but the illustrious can satisfy the wishes of the worthy. The ocean alone supports the sub-terrestrial flame."

The Yogi, finding them apt scholars, admitted their request, and gave them four magical balls, one a piece, directing them to go to the northern side of the Himachala mountains, where each, on the spot where the balls should spontaneously fall, would find a treasure. They accordingly went thither, and one of the balls soon fell on the ground. The Brahman to whom it belonged, with the assistance of the rest, dug up the soil, and there discovered a copper mine. He desired the others to take as much as they liked, but they refused, determining to seek their fortunes farther. He replied, "Go on then, I shall return." Taking, therefore, as much of the metal as he could, he went back, and the others proceeded on their way.

The ball belonging to another soon fell, and he dug up the spot, which proved to contain a silver mine. Overjoyed, he exclaimed, "Let us go no farther, but take as much as we can, and then return." The other two, however, ridiculed his folly, and resolved to advance, hoping, as they had rst met with copper and then silver, they should successively meet with metal still more valuable. So it proved, for the next ball that fell indicated a vein of gold. The man to whom the ball belonged entreated his companion to rest satisfied. The argument previously used, however, being justified by the discovery of gold, determined him to persevere, in the full confidence that he should next come to a bed of diamonds. The discoverer of the gold mine declined to accompany him, and he went on alone, the other promising to await his return.

The last Brahman proceeded through solitary paths, scorched by the rays of the sun, and faint with thirst, till at last he came to a place which was whirling round, and on it stood a man, whose body was covered with blood, and on whose head a wheel revolved. He approached and asked him who he was, and why the wheel was placed upon his head, and requested him also to show him where any water was procurable; but he had scarcely spoken when the wheel transferred itself from the crown of its late possessor to the head of the Brahman. He exclaimed, "How! What is this?" And the stranger replied, "You have taken the wheel from my head, and you must keep it, till some one, like yourself, shall come hither with that magic ball in his hand, and shall address to you similar questions to those you have asked of me." The Brahman inquired how long a time he had passed in that plight. The stranger asked, "Who was the present sovereign?" To which the Brahman answered, "Vinà Vatsa." The man then said: "When Rama reigned I came hither, impelled by my poverty, and guided by the magic ball as thou hast been. I found a man here with the wheel upon his head, and asking him the same questions as thou hast put, the wheel was fixed upon my head.

I have been here ever since." "And how did you get anything to eat," inquired the Brahman? The other replied: "This law was fixed by the God of Wealth, who fears his treasures should be plundered. His fears are known to the Siddhi Nagas, who send men hither, but when a mortal arrives he loses the sensation of hunger and thirst, and is exempt from decay and death. He retains alone the consciousness of solitude and pain. But now excuse me, I am released, and shall return home." So saying, he departed.

The Brahman who had found the gold mine wondered why his companion tarried so long, and becoming at last impatient, he set off in quest of him. Tracing his course by the impressions of his feet he followed him to the spot where he stood, and beheld him covered with blood, running down from his head, which was cut by the sharp edges of the wheel. To the inquiries of his friend he replied by telling him the property of the wheel, and what had happened to himself. On which the other reproached him, saying, "Did I not tell you to stop? but your lack of sense would not allow you to take my advice. It is very justly observed, 'Better sense than science, unless it improve by knowledge.' Those who want common understanding will as surely perish as did those who revived the lion." The man with the wheel asked how that was, to which the other replied:

"There were four Brahmans residing in the same village, all intimate friends. Three of them were men of great acquirements, but destitute of common sense. The fourth was an intelligent fellow, but destitute of learning. As they were poor, they determined at one of their meetings to go to some country where learning was patronized, and where they were satisfied that they would speedily be enriched with presents from the King. They accordingly set off, but when they had gone some way the eldest cried out, 'It never occurred to me before that our fourth friend here is illiterate. He is a man of sense to be sure, but that will not entitle him to any rewards from the King; we shall have, therefore, to relinquish to him a part of our earnings, and it would be fairer, I think, for him to remain at home.' The second agreed in this opinion, but the third opposed it, saying, 'We have always been friends and companions from infancy, and let him therefore participate in the wealth we shall acquire.' This sentiment prevailed, and they all went on in harmony. As they passed through a forest they saw the scattered bones of a dead lion. 'I have met,' said one, 'with an account of a method by which beings can be re-animated. What say you? shall we try the experiment, and employ the energies of science to restore life and shape to these bones?' They agreed. One undertook to put the bones together, the second to supply the skin, flesh, blood, &c., and the other to communicate life to the figure. When the two first had accomplished their tasks, the third was about to begin his, but the fourth stopped him. 'Consider what you are going to do,' he exclaimed; 'if you give life to the lion, the consequence will be that he will devour us.' 'Away, blockhead,' replied the sage, 'I am not to project things in vain.' 'Wait an instant, then,' replied the man of sense, 'till I get up into this tree.' So saying, he climbed up into a tree at hand, and his learned associates accomplished their undertaking. A substantial living lion was formed, who fell upon the three philosophers and destroyed them. When the lion had departed, the man of common sense descended from his hiding-place, and reached his home again in safety."

When he had finished, the man with the wheel exclaimed, "It is very unreasonable that destiny should destroy men of great talents, and allow simpletons to escape, as it is said: 'See where Satabuddhi or the hundred-witted one is carried on the head, and there also is Sahasrabuddhi or the thousand-witted one, whilst I, who am Ekabuddhi or the single-wit, still can gambol in the crystal stream.'" "How," asked he of the gold mine, "did that happen?" The man with the wheel replied:

"In a certain reservoir were two fishes, one named Satabuddhi, the other Sahasrabuddhi. They had a friend, a frog, named Ekabuddhi, with whom they were in the habit of meeting and conversing at the edge of the water. When the usual party assembled, they saw several fishermen approach with their nets, and heard them say to one another, 'This pool is full of fish, the water is but shallow; we will come to-morrow morning and drag it.' They then went away. When they had departed the frog said to his friends, 'What is to be done, had we not better make our escape?' at which the thousand-witted laughed and said, 'Never fear, they have only talked of coming. Yet if they should come I will be answerable for your safety as well as my own. I shall be a match for them, as I know all the courses of the water.' The hundred-witted one said, 'My friend here is very right; wherever there is a way for the breeze, for water or its tenants, or for the rays of the sun, the intellect of a sagacious person will penetrate. By following his counsel your life would be in no peril, even had you approached the abodes of the manes. Stay where you are, even I will undertake your safety.' The frog said, 'I have perhaps but limited talent, a mere singleness of sense, but that tells me to flee, and therefore whilst I can I shall withdraw with my mate to another piece of water.' The frog left the pool that night. In the morning the fishermen arrived, and the lake was so beset with nets that all the fish, turtles, crabs, and other tenants of the water, were made prisoners, and amongst them Satabuddhi and Sahasrabuddhi, in spite of their boasted cunning, were caught and killed. The frog saw the fishermen on their return, and recognizing Satabuddhi on the head of one man, and Sahasrabuddhi dragged along with cords by another, he pointed them out to his mate, in the words which I cited."

The Brahman of the gold mine answered, "This may be very true, but a friend's words are not to be despised, and you had better have listened to me than followed the dictates of your own avarice and presumption. Well was it said, 'Bravo, uncle; you would sing your song though I dissuaded you, and see what a splendid gem you have received as the recompense of your performance.'" The man with the wheel asked, "How was that?" The other replied:

"In a certain village there was an ass named Uddhata. During the day he carried the bundles of a washerman; at night he followed his own inclinations. During his nocturnal rambles he made acquaintance with a jackal, in whose company he broke into enclosures, and feasted on their contents. On one occasion, when in the middle of a cucumber field, the ass exulting with delight, said to the jackal, 'Nephew, is not this an heavenly night? I feel so happy that I must sing a song; in what key will you prefer it?' The jackal replied, 'What nonsense, when we are engaged in plundering, to think of such a thing. Silence becomes thieves and libertines, as it is said, "Let the sick man and the lazy man refrain from stealing and chattering if they would escape with life." If your song be ever so sweet, should the owner of the field hear you, he will rise, and in his rage will bind and kill you; eat, therefore, and be silent.' The ass replied, 'You can be no judge of the charms of music, as you have spent all your life in the woods. Observe in the nights of autumn, in privacy with your love, the distant song of the singer drops like nectar into the ears.' The jackal answered, 'It may be so, but your voice is abominable; why should you let it lead you into trouble?' The ass was highly affronted at this, and said, 'Away, blockhead, do you question my musical proficiency? I know every branch of the science; for instance, there are seven notes, three scales, and twenty-one intervals. The scientific combination of the parts of music is particularly grateful in the autumnal season. There is no gift of the gods more precious than music. Rávána received the boon from the three-eyed god (Siva). How, then, do you presume to question my powers, or to oppose their exercise?' 'Very well,' replied the jackal, 'let me get to the door of the garden, where I may see the gardener as he approaches, and then sing away as long as you please.' So it was settled, and the jackal having provided for his own safety, the ass opened his chaunt. The gardener was awakened by the noise, and, rising immediately, repaired to the spot, armed with a stout stick, with which he fell upon the ass, knocked him down, and belaboured him till he was tired. He then brought a large clog with a hole in it, which he fastened to his leg, and tied him to a post, after which he returned home, and went to sleep. The ass came to himself, and forgot his tortures in the recollection of his home and companions. As it is said, 'On a dog, a mule, and an ass, a good beating leaves but a momentary impression.' Accordingly, springing up, he forced his way out of the enclosure, carrying his clog with him. As he ran off, the jackal met him, and said, 'Bravo, uncle, you would sing your song, though I dissuaded you, and see what you have received as the recompense of your performance.'"

The man with the wheel having heard this story, answered, "What you observe is very just; but you should recollect that a man who neither exercises his own judgment, nor follows a friend's advice, brings on his own ruin, as was the case with Manthara, the weaver.

"There was once a weaver named Manthara, all the woodwork of whose loom was on one occasion broken. Taking his axe, he set off to cut fresh timber, and finding a large Sisu tree by the sea-side, began to fell it. In the tree resided a spirit, who exclaimed, on the first stroke of the axe, 'Hold, this tree is my dwelling, and I cannot quit it, as here I inhale the fresh breeze that is cooled by the ocean's spray.' The weaver replied, 'What am I to do? unless I get wood my family must starve. Do you therefore look out for another house; quick, this I must have.' The spirit replied, 'You shall have anything else you ask for, but not this tree.' The weaver then agreed to go home and consult a friend and his wife, and return with his final determination.

"When the weaver returned home, he found there a very particular friend of his, the barber of the village, to whom he told what had occurred, and whom he consulted what he should request. The barber said, 'Ask to be made a king, then I will be your prime minister, and we shall enjoy ourselves gloriously.' The weaver approved of his idea, but first, he said, he must consult his wife. To this the barber strenuously objected. 'A wise man,' he argued, 'would confer on woman food, clothing, and appropriate ornaments, but would never let them share his councils, as Bhágava has stated, that where a woman, a rogue, or a child had the management, the house was sure of going to ruin. A man would maintain his rank and respectability as long as he associated with grave people, and entrusted no woman with his secrets. Women are engrossed with their own designs, and purpose only their own pleasure. They love their own children even no longer than they derive from them self-gratification.' The weaver admitted the justice of his friend's observations, but his wife, he said, had no other thoughts than for her husband's welfare, and he must take her advice. Accordingly, he went to her and related what had happened, what the barber had recommended, and asked her what she thought it would be most advantageous for him to solicit. She replied:

"'You should never listen, husband, to the advice of a barber, as it is said, "Husbands should never take counsel with courtezans, parasites, mean persons, barbers, gardeners, and beggars." Royalty is a very troublesome thing, and the cares of peace and war, aggression and negotiation, defence and administration, never allow its possessor a moment's enjoyment. He who is wise will ever shun the station of a king, for which his own relations, brothers and offspring, would be armed against his life. I should recommend you, therefore, to be contented with your station, and only to seek the means of more effectually earning your livelihood. Ask for an additional pair of hands, and another head with which you may keep a loom going both before and behind you. The profit of such a second loom will be quiet sufficient to give you consequence and credit with your tribe, as we have already from the profit of the first loom quite enough for our own expenditure.'

"This advice pleased the husband mightily. He repaired forthwith to the tree and requested the spirit, as the price of his forbearance to give him another pair of arms and an additional head. No sooner said than done; and he immediately found himself in possession of two heads and four arms, with which he returned homewards highly delighted. His new acquisition, however, proved fatal, for as soon as the villagers saw him, they exclaimed, 'a goblin! a goblin!' and falling on him with clubs or pelting him with stones, speedily put an end to his existence. Therefore I say that a man who neither exercises his own judgment nor follows a friend's advice brings on his own ruin."

The man with the wheel continued, "Every one who is tormented by the devil of improper expectations naturally incurs ridicule, as it is said, 'He who forms extravagant hopes for the future, will be as much disappointed as the father of Soma Sarma.'" "How was that?" asked the other Brahman, and he with the wheel proceeded:

"There was an avaricious Brahman named Soma Sarma, who had collected, during the days, in alms as much meal as filled an earthen jar. This jar he suspended to a peg at the foot of his bed, so that he might not lose sight of it. During the night he lay awake some time, and reflected thus—'That jar is full of meal; if a scarcity should take place, I shall sell it for a hundred pieces at least. With that sum I will buy a pair of goats, they will bear young, and I shall get enough by their sale to purchase a pair of cows. I shall sell their calves, and will purchase buffaloes, and with the produce of my herd I shall be able to buy horses and mares. By the sale of their colts I shall realize an immense sum, and with my money I will build a stately mansion. As I shall then be a man of consequence, some wealthy person will solicit my acceptance of his daughter with a suitable dower. I shall have a son by her, whom I will call by my own name, Soma Sarma. When he is able to crawl, I shall take him with me on my horse, seating him before me. Accordingly, when Soma Sarma sees me, he will leave his mother's lap, and come creeping along, and some day or other he will approach the horses too near, when I shall be very angry, and shall desire his mother to take him away. She will be busy with her household duties, and will not hear my orders, on which I shall give her a kick with my foot.' Thus saying, he put forth one of his feet with such violence as to break the jar. The meal accordingly fell on the ground, where, mingling with the dust and dirt, it was completely spoiled, and so ended Soma Sarma's hopes."

After some further conversation, the Brahman of the gold mine finally tells the following tale:—

"There is a city in the north named Madhupura, of which Madhusena was king. A daughter was born to him who had three breasts. When the king heard this, he ordered the chief attendant to take away the infant and expose her in the woods, so that the matter should remain unknown. The attendant, however, recommended that as the birth of such an infant was such an extraordinary event, it would be better to consult the Brahmans what was to be done, so that the consequence might not be the loss of both worlds; as it is said, 'A wise man should always inquire the meaning of what he observes,' like the Brahman who thus escaped the grasp of the goblin. The king asked how that was, to which the attendant replied:

"'Chandavarma, a Rákshasa, or goblin, haunted a certain wood, and one day laid hold of a Brahman who passed that way, and leaping upon his shoulders, ordered him to proceed. The Brahman, overcome with terror, obeyed; but as he went along, he observed that the goblin's feet were particularly soft and tender, and inquired of him how this happened. The Rákshasa replied, "I was under a vow never to walk or touch the ground with my feet." After this they came to a pool where the Rákshasa said, "Let me down whilst I bathe and perform my devotions; but beware how you leave the place till I come out of the water." The Brahman obeyed, but when he had got rid of his load he reflected that now was his time to escape, for as the Rákshasa was incapacitated for walking, he would not be able to overtake the fugitive; accordingly he took to his heels, and effected his retreat in safety. Therefore I said a wise man should always inquire the meaning of what he observes.'

"The advice thus given by the attendant was followed by the Raja, and having summoned the Brahmans, he consulted them how he should act, to which they replied, 'It is said, sire, that a daughter whose limbs are defective or excessive will be the cause of death to her husband, and of destruction to her own character; and a damsel with three breasts will inevitably be the source of evil to the parent whose sight she may attract. Your majesty should therefore take care to avoid seeing your daughter. Let any one that will, marry her, you stipulating that he leaves the country. In this way no offence will be offered either to this world or the next.' The Raja approved of this plan, and ordered the drum to be beat and a proclamation to be made that whoever would marry the princess, and remove with her to a distant country, should receive a hundred thousand rupees. Notwithstanding this offer no person came forward, and the princess arrived at adolescence without any one proposing to espouse her. At last she found a husband.

"In the city resided two paupers who were friends; the one was blind, and the other hunch-backed; the latter, who was named Manthara, persuaded the former to marry the princess, with whom and with the money they should remove to a distant place, and lead a life of ease; or if by the evil nature of the princess he should die, there would at least be an end of his misery. The blind man accordingly accepted the terms of the proclamation, and having married the princess, and received the dower, set off with her and his friend to a distant residence.

"After passing some time contentedly, the blind man giving himself up to indolence, and hunch-back conducting their domestic arrangements, the evil influence of the princess's deformity began to operate, and she intrigued with hunchback. This couple then soon began to plot the blind man's destruction. With this intent, hunchback brought home one day a dead snake of a venomous nature, which he gave to the princess, and desired her to mince it, and dress it with proper sauces, after which she should give it to her husband, telling him it was a dish of fish. Manthara then went away, and the princess, delighted, cut up the snake, and set it to boil; then having other matters to look after, she called to her husband, and desired him to attend to the stirring of the nice mess of fish she was cooking for his dinner. He obeyed her, licking his lips at the intimation, and stirring the vessel as it boiled. In this manner, hanging over the caldron, the fumes of the venom drew the tears so copiously from his eyes that they gradually dissolved the film which obscured his vision, and he was restored to sight. As he looked into the boiler, he saw immediately that he was cooking the fragments of a black snake. He at once concluded what his wife's design was, but remained in doubt who her accomplice could be. To ascertain this, he resolved to dissemble, and still affect his former blindness. Presently hunchback returned, and the husband, watching his conduct unobserved, was soon satisfied of the good understanding that subsisted between the treacherous friend and the faithless spouse. He approached them unperceived, and suddenly seizing hunchback by the feet, being a man of great strength, he whirled him over his head, and dashed him against the breast of the wife with such violence that his head drove her third breast through her body to her back, and both she and her paramour instantly perished."

The Brahman who had found the gold mine then concluded: "It is well said, 'All prosperity proceeds from Fate'; but, in compliance with Destiny, Prudence is not to be disregarded in the manner in which you neglected it by not listening to my advice." He then left his friend to his fate, and returned to his own abode.

CHAPTER II.

OF THE HITOPODESA, OR FRIENDLY ADVICE.

THE Pancha Tantra is followed in Sanscrit literature by the Hitopodesa, or Friendly Advice, a selection of tales drawn from the same source, but not so voluminous, or arranged in the same order. Written in prose and verse, the exact date or name of the author cannot be fixed; but it is described as follows, in the title-page of the translation by Francis Johnson:—

"Hitopodesa, or Salutary Counsels of Vishnu Sarman, in a Series of Connected Fables, interspersed with Moral, Prudential, and Political Maxims, translated literally from the original into English for the use of the Sanscrit student." The work had been previously translated by Dr. Charles Wilkins and Sir William Jones, but Johnson's production is the most satisfactory, as it lays before the reader, in fulness and exactness, a vivid picture of the Sanscrit original. Full of maxims and worldly advice, it is as interesting as the Proverbs or Ecclesiastes, and probably as old as those works. Opening with a reverence to Ganesa, the Hindoo god of wisdom, it commences, like the Book of Common Prayer, with a series of serious verses, and then goes on with the text, which may be briefly analyzed as follows:—

In the city of Pataliputra there reigned a king, by name Sudarsana, whose sons caused him much anxiety from their ignorance and wickedness.

Thinking how he could render them accomplished, and also keep them in the right path, he caused an assembly of learned men to be called together, and addressed them: "O Pandits, be it heard. Is there any one so learned who is able now, by instruction in books of policy, to effect the new birth of my sons, ever following wrong courses, and unread in the learned writings. For,

"'Glass, from the contiguity of gold, acquires an emerald lustre; so by the proximity of the excellent, a fool attains to cleverness.' And it is said,

"'The mind is lowered from association with inferiors. With equals it attains equality, and with superiors, superiority.'" On this a great Pandit, by name Vishnu Sarman, undertook to complete the education of the young princes, and in the period of six months to make them versed in the works of policy. To this the king assented, and Vishnu Sarman commenced his instructions in the shape of tales, divided into four chapters; the first on the acquisition of friends, the second on the separation of friends, the third on war, and the fourth on peace. As is often the custom in oriental literature, one story is commenced, but, owing to some allusion in it, another story is interpolated, as it were, into it, and when this is finished, the original tale is reverted to, only to be again interrupted with another one, and so on. Each story, in addition to its regular text, is padded with maxims, happy thoughts, and truisms, which swell its length considerably. As they are all much of a muchness in quality, it is difficult to make any particular selection, but the following will serve as specimens of the work:—

THE CROW, THE GOLDEN CHAIN, AND THE SERPENT.

In a certain tree lived a male and female crow, whose young ones were devoured by a black serpent that lurked within its hollow trunk. Finding herself breeding again, the female crow thus addressed her mate: "My dear, let this tree be forsaken; for as long as this black serpent remains here, we shall never rear any offspring. For,

"'A termagant wife, a false friend, a servant that gives saucy answers, and a residence in a house infested by serpents, is death beyond a doubt.'"

"My beloved," said the crow, "there is no cause for alarm. Time after time, this enormous offence of his has been borne by me; but now it is to be endured no longer." "How," inquired the female, "are you able to contend with this powerful black serpent?" "Away," replied the crow, "with apprehensions of this kind. For,

"'He who hath sense, hath strength, but whence hath a fool strength?' See how a lion, intoxicated with pride, was defeated by a rabbit." "How was that?" said the female. The crow related:

"Upon a mountain called Mandara there was a lion, by name Durdanta (hard to tame), who was for ever making a massacre of the beasts. At length the lion was thus respectfully remonstrated with by all the beasts forming a meeting: 'Please, your highness, wherefore is a general carnage of the beasts made? We will ourselves, as a free gift, daily furnish a single beast for your honour's meal.' 'If this is agreeable to you,' said the lion, 'then be it so;' and thenceforward he used daily to eat the single allotted beast. On a certain day, the turn of an old rabbit being come, he thought to himself:

"'Through fear, homage is paid in the hope of

life; but if I must meet this fate, why need I cringe to the lion? Then I will approach him very leisurely.'

"The lion being by this time tormented with hunger, called out to him in a rage, 'Wherefore comest thou after so much delay?' The rabbit replied, 'I am not in fault, for on the road I was forcibly detained by another lion, but having made an oath before him to return, I am come here to inform my lord.' The lion, with anger, exclaimed, 'Go quickly, and show me where that vile wretch is to be found.' The rabbit then taking him, came near a deep well, and after saying, 'Let my lord come here and see,' he showed him his own image reflected in the water of the well; whereupon being inflated with pride, he threw himself upon it and perished. Therefore, I say, he who hath sense," &c.

"I have attentively listened," said the hen crow; "declare what is to be done." "My dear," said the crow, "the Raja's son comes daily and bathes in the adjacent pool. With thy beak having seized the chain of gold when taken from off his person, and laid on that stone, thou must bring it and place it in this hollow trunk." Accordingly some time afterwards, as soon as the Raja's son had entered the water to bathe, after laying the chain of gold on the rock, the plan was executed by the hen crow; and, the black serpent being discovered in the hollow of the tree by the Raja's servants as they were engaged in searching for the golden chain, was put to death. Wherefore, I say, "That may be effected by stratágem, which could not be accomplished by force."

THE BLUE JACKAL.

A certain jackal, as he roamed for his pleasure on the outskirts of a town, fell into an indigo vat;

and being unable afterwards to rise, in the morning he lay still, making himself appear as if dead. Then the owner of the indigo vat, having lifted him out and carried him to a distance, left him. He afterwards ran off to the wood; and perceiving himself to be of a blue colour, he thus reflected: I am now of the finest colour; may I not then effect my own exaltation? Saying which, he summoned the jackals and said to them: "With an extract of every medicinal plant have I been anointed to the sovereignty of the forest by the adorable divinity of the wood with her own hand. Behold my colour! Beginning, therefore, from to-day, all business must be transacted in this forest by my order." The jackals seeing him of such a distinguished colour, said, as they reverentially prostrated themselves, "As your Majesty commands." By this means his sovereignty was established over all the inhabitants of the forest; and his power was extended still further by him, while surrounded by his own kindred. But afterwards, when he had procured attendants of a higher grade, such as lions, tigers, and the like, he looked down upon the jackals, and having treated them with disrespect, his own relations were removed to a distance, as he was ashamed of them. Then perceiving the jackals to be afflicted, an old jackal made a promise: "Be not grieved, although we who knew him thoroughly are treated with contempt by this imprudent kinsman. I must so contrive that he perish. Since the tigers and the rest are deceived solely by his colour, and not knowing him to be a jackal fancy him a king; therefore do something that he may be detected. Let it then be done, according as I say. In the evening you will all at once set up a great yell near him; then when he hears that noise he will naturally make a cry also. For the natural disposition of any one, whatever it may be, is hard to be overcome by him. If a dog were made king, would he not gnaw his shoe strap? The tiger then discovering him by his voice will kill him."

This plan being carried into execution, the predicted result came to pass. Thus it has been said:

"Our natural enemy knows every weak point, our heart and courage, and having gotten within consumes us, as fire does a dry tree:

"Wherefore I say: By deserting his own party, and attaching himself to the opposite party, the blockhead is killed by the strangers, like the blue jackal."

THE OLD SERPENT AND THE FROGS.

In an uncultivated garden, there was a serpent called Mauda-visarpa (slow-glide), who through extreme old age, being unable to seek food for himself, laid himself down on the edge of a pond, where from a distance he was seen by a certain frog, and questioned: "How is it you do not ply for food?" "Hear me, worthy sir, "said the serpent; "what hast thou to do with inquiries into the story of a hapless wretch like me?" Upon this the frog, not a little pleased, said to the serpent: "Tell it by all means." The serpent said: "Good sir, here in Brahmepura, the son of one Kaundinya, a learned Brahman, about twenty years old, and endued with every good quality, through evil destiny, was bitten by cruel me. Kaundinya seeing his son, Susila (amiable) by name, dead, became senseless with grief, and rolled on the ground. Thereupon all his kinsmen, inhabitants of Brahmepura, having come to the place, sat down. For thus it has been said: 'He is a kinsman who attends upon one at an invitation to a feast, and also in affliction;

in a famine, in a contest with an enemy, at the king's gate, and at the cemetery.'

"Then spake a householder, Kapila by name: "O Kaundinya! Thou art beside thyself since thou complainest thus. Listen.

"As this transient state of being only folds you to her bosom, as the nurse or mother folds the newly born child, what cause is there then for grief?

"In like manner:

"Where are those rulers of the earth gone with their guards, armies and carriages, of whose departure the earth stands a witness unto the present day.

"Again:

"This body wasting away every moment, is not perceived to decay like a jar of unbaked clay standing in water; its dissolution is known when it has been dissolved.

"Day by day, death approaches nearer and nearer a living being, as to a victim being led step by step to the slaughter.

"For:

"Youth, beauty, life, a store of worldly goods, dominion, the society of friends, are all uncertain: by these a wise man should not be beguiled.

"As a plank of timber may meet with another plank in the mighty receptacle of waters, and having met, may again separate; even such is the meeting of human beings.

"As a traveller halts, taking refuge in the shade, and having reposed awhile resumes his journey, such is the meeting of animated beings.

"Moreover:

"What occasion is there for lamentation over a body composed of five elements returning to its five original principles, and finding again its own birth-place?

"How many soever connexions dear to the soul a living being forms, so many thorns of sorrow are implanted in his heart.

"For union denotes the existence of separation, as birth implies the approach of death, which is not to be avoided.

"As the streams of rivers flow onwards and return not, so do night and day pass on for ever, carrying off the life of mortals.

"The very first night on which the man of valour took up his abode in the womb, thenceforwards without faltering in his march, he approaches death day by day."

"Form, then, a just estimate of mundane existence. This sorrow is an illusion of ignorance. Therefore, good sir, compose thyself, and dismiss all thought of sorrow."

On hearing his address, Kaundinya, awakening as it were from a trance, cried out, as he started up, "Enough now of dwelling in a hell of a house, I will go to the forest."

Kapila then continues with further admonitions and consolations, to which Kaundinya assented. "After that," continued the serpent, "I was cursed by that disconsolate Brahman in the following terms: 'Beginning this day thou shalt become a carrier of frogs.' Kaundinya, the fire of whose grief was now extinguished by the nectar of the instruction of Kapila, then assumed the pilgrim's staff according to the sacred ordinances, and here I wait to endure the Brahman's curse to carry frogs." Then that frog went and reported it to Webfoot, the chief of his race, who, having come himself, mounted upon the serpent. The serpent having taken him, on his back, made a little excursion at an agreeable pace. Next day the prince of the frogs said to him as he lay scarcely able to move: "How is it you are so sluggish to-day"? "Please, your Majesty," replied the serpent, "I am weak for want of food." "Eat the frogs by my command," said their monarch, to which the serpent replied: "This great favour is thankfully accepted;" saying which, he ate the frogs by degrees, until seeing the pond cleared of its frogs, he swallowed his Majesty likewise. Wherefore I say—

"A wise man having an object in view, should carry even his enemies on his shoulder, as the frogs were destroyed by the old serpent."

THE BRAHMAN AND HIS WEASEL.

In Oujein lived a Brahman named Madhara. His wife, of the Brahmanical tribe, who had recently brought forth, went to perform her ablutions, leaving him to take charge of her infant offspring. Presently a person from the Raja came for the Brahman to perform for him a religious ceremony. When the Brahman saw him, being impelled by his natural poverty, he thought within himself: "If I go not directly, then some one else will take the fee for the ceremony. It is said:

"'In respect of a thing which ought to be taken, or to be given, or of a work which ought to be done, and not being done quickly, time drinks up the spirit thereof.'

"But there is no one here to take care of the child: what can I do, then? Well, I will go, having set to guard the infant this weasel, cherished a long time, and in no respect distinguished from a child of my own." This he did, and went. Shortly afterwards a black serpent, whilst silently coming near the child, was killed there, and rent in pieces by the weasel, who seeing the Brahman coming home, ran towards him with haste, his mouth and hands all smeared with blood, and rolled himself at his feet. The Brahman seeing him in that state, without reflecting said, "My son has been eaten by the weasel," and killed him; but as soon as he drew near and looked, behold the child was comfortably sleeping, and the serpent lay killed. Thereupon the Brahman was overwhelmed with grief. Wherefore I say that the blockhead who, without knowing the true state of the case, becomes subject to anger, will have cause for regret in the same manner as the Brahman on account of the weasel.

In conclusion some of the maxims, as given in the work in the shape of verses, have been selected and arranged under such separate English headings as may be applicable to them.

Concealment.

Nine things ought carefully to be concealed: age, wealth, domestic troubles, private counsel, conjugal rites, medicine, penance, almsgiving, and disgrace.

A prudent person should not publish the loss of property, distress of mind, mal-practices in his house, his being cozened, and his disgrace.

Confidence.

Confidence ought never to be put in rivers; in those with weapons in their hands, in animals having claws or horns, in women, and in king's families.

Contentment.

Whoever has a contented mind, has all riches. To him whose foot is enclosed in a shoe, is it not as though the earth were carpeted with leather?

Where have they, who greedy of wealth, are running here and there, the happiness which those placid spirits enjoy, who are satisfied with the nectar of contentment?

Covetousness.

From covetousness anger proceeds, from covetousness lust is born, from covetousness comes delusion and perdition. Covetousness is the cause of sin.

Existence.

The difference between the body and the qualities of the mind is infinitely wide. The body is extinct in a moment, whilst the qualities endure to the end of creation.

Feelings.

Is this one of your tribe or a stranger is the calculation of the narrow-minded, but to those of a noble disposition the earth itself is but one family.

As the feelings of those pinched with cold take no pleasure in the rays of the moon; nor of those oppressed with heat in the beams of the sun, so the heart of women delights not in a husband stricken with old age.

When grey hairs have appeared what, forsooth, is a man's love? since women having their hearts fixed on others, regard him as a drug.

The lust of wealth, and the love of life in living beings, is ever strong, but a youthful wife is dearer to an old man than life itself.

A decrepit old man can neither enjoy nor relinquish the pleasures of sense, as a toothless dog only licks a bone with his tongue.

The man of fine feelings dies without reluctance, but submits not to penury. Fire, though it may be extinguished, will not be cooled.

Fortune, Goddess of.

As a young woman loves not to embrace an old

husband, so Lakshmi, the Goddess of Fortune, loves not to embrace the inactive, the lazy, the fatalist, or the coward.

Friendship.

In this life there is none more happy than he who has a friend to converse with, a friend to live with, and a friend to chat with.

A friend who is so by nature, is produced by good fortune; his unfeigned friendship he renounces not, even in imminent danger.

Not in a mother, not in a wife, not in a whole brother, nor in a son, have men such confidence as in the friend who is produced by conformity of disposition.

That friend who will be to his friend an elixir of joy for the eyes, the delight of the heart, a repository of pleasure and pain, is hard to be acquired; whilst such others as, being filled with a desire of gain, are friends in his season of prosperity everywhere abound. Adversity is the touchstone of their principles.

Government.

When a government is deserted by the wise, the administration becomes unsound; the administration being inefficient, the whole being without control, declines.

Greatness.

Idleness, devotion to women, sickness, a fondness for one's native place, contentment and timidity, are obstacles to greatness.

Kings, Duty of.

A king who understands the principles of duty, interest and pleasure, should not be over-merciful, for one over-lenient is not able to keep his property, although within his grasp.

Forgiveness of a foe as well as of a friend is doubtless the ornament of religious men, when extended to offending beings, in a monarch it is a fault.

For him who, through the lust of power or through pride, is aspiring to his master's station, forfeiture of life is the only expiation; there is no other.

A king over-merciful, a Brahman who eats all things alike, a disobedient wife, an ill-natured companion, an unruly servant, a negligent officer, and one who acknowledges not a benefit received, these ought to be avoided.

The policy of princes, like a harlot, assumes various forms, true and false, harsh and courteous, cruel and merciful, niggardly and generous, always spending and still intent on ample hoards of jewels and money.

If there were no king, or competent leader, then would the people be tossed about here like a ship at sea without a steersman.

Moral Maxims.

Shun the society of the wicked. Cultivate the society of the good. Practise virtue day and night. Remember always your transient state.

Passion.

Passion should be relinquished with all the soul, but, if it cannot be given up, it should be indulged towards one's own wife, for she is the proper remedy for it.

Philosophy.

Philosophic-minded men hanker not after what is unattainable, are not inclined to grieve for what is lost, nor are they perplexed even in calamities.

He, by whom swans were formed white, parrots

made green, and peacocks painted of various hues, will make a provision for thee.

Poverty.

Empty is the house of a childless man, and of him who is destitute of a true friend. Empty are all quarters of the world to an ignorant man. Poverty is total emptiness.

Of poverty, or of death, poverty is declared the worst. Death is attended with transient pain, poverty is past endurance.

From poverty he comes to shame; overwhelmed with shame, he loses spirit; broken in spirit he is despised; through contempt he proceeds to self-disparagement; self-disparaged he sinks into melancholy; sorrow-stricken he is forsaken by reason; deprived of reason he goes to destruction. Alas, poverty is the seat of all calamities.

Providence or Destiny.

Whoever with a very moderate fortune thinks himself well off, I expect Providence, which does all it ought to do, will not increase it for him.

The allotted age preserves the vital parts of one plunged in the ocean, fallen from a precipice, or bitten by a serpent.

Though pierced by hundreds of arrows at the wrong time, an animal dies not; touched but by the point of a blade of grass, if he has reached his hour, he lives no longer.

An object unguarded, continues safe if guarded by destiny; though well guarded, if stricken by destiny it perishes. One turned adrift in a forest without a protector lives; another, though using every precaution at home, lives not.

Qualities of Character.

In adversity, fortitude; in prosperity, moderation; in the assembly, eloquence; in war, valour; ambition for fame; perseverance in study; this is perfect in the nature of the high-minded.

Rarely does a mother bring forth that son, an ornament to the three worlds of whom there is neither exultation in prosperity, nor dejection in adversity, and in battle steadfastness.

Well water, the shade of a bata tree, a brunette, and a brick house, should be warm in cold weather, and cool in warm weather.

Queries.

What is religion? tenderness towards all creatures. What is happiness? to a living being in this world it is health. What is kindness? a benevolent disposition. What is learning? Judgment.

Science.

What can science do for him who has no sense of his own? What will a mirror do for one without eyes?

Truth.

If a thousand sacrifices of a horse and truth were weighed in a balance, truth would certainly be of more weight than a thousand sacrifices of a horse.

Utility.

A horse, a weapon, a book, a lute, a speech, a man, and a woman become serviceable or useless according as they belong to varieties of men.

What benefit accrues by one who is faithful, but without ability? or what benefit by one who is able, but hostile? I, who am faithful and able, O king, thou oughtest not to despise.

Ways of Reception.

With money one should receive a covetous man; with hands joined in token of respect, a haughty man; with the humouring of his wishes, a blockhead; and with truth a clever man.

One should receive a friend with kindness, kinsmen with lively emotion, women and servants with gifts and honour, and other people with courtesy.

Wealth.

In this world every wealthy man is everywhere and at all times strong. Even the power of kings arises based on wealth. With wealth every one is powerful; through wealth one becomes learned.

He who has riches has friends; he who has riches has relations; he who has riches is a man of consequence in the world; he who has riches is even a sage.

Wisdom.

He who looks on the wife of another as a mother, on the goods of another as a clod of earth, and on all creatures as himself, is a wise man.

Wishes.

Whatever a man may wish for, after that his desire still progresses. That object is virtually obtained the desire for which has ceased.

Women.

Absolute liberty; a residence in her father's house; attendance at festivals; the absence of restraint in the neighbourhood of distant male relations; living in a foreign country; frequent intercourse with loose women; waste of her substance; the old age of a husband; the envied fecundity of other women are the cause of the ruin of a woman.

Drinking; bad company; absence from her husband; gadding about; much sleep; dwelling in another's house, are six things injurious to women.

It is notorious that women have ever been inconstant, even among the celestials. And fortunate, indeed, are those men whose wives are kept from error.

A woman is like a pot of ghee, and a man is like a burning coal. A prudent person, therefore, should not put the ghee and the fire together.

In childhood the father guards her; in youth, the husband guards her; and in old age her sons should take care of her. A woman is not fit for independence.

Every book of knowledge which Usanas knows, and which Vrihaspati knows, is by nature already implanted in the understanding of women.

And then comes the last verse.

May peace and happiness ever be the portion of all victorious monarchs! May the good be exempt from misfortune! May the glory of those who perform great deeds long increase! May policy, like a wanton, closely cling to the breast, and kiss the lips of statesmen! Day by day may great joy be to all!

CHAPTER III.

OF THE KATHASARITSAGARA, ALIAS VRIHATKATHA-SAGARA, OR VRIHATKATHA.

THE next well-known work is the Kathásaritságara, or ocean of the streams of narrative, or watery ocean of stories. It is more commonly known in India as the Vrihatkathá, the great tale, or great collection of tales, from which the former work has been compiled. The date and author of the Vrihatkathá are both unknown, but it was written in prose in minute detail, while the Kathásaritságara, which is more compressed in style, was written in verse by one Bhatta Somadeva in the eleventh century, say A.D. 1088. It is a large work, and consists of eighteen books, subdivided into 124 sections, and a portion of it only has been translated. The first book is introductory, and refers the origin of the stories contained in the collection to no less a person than the deity Siva, who told them to his wife Purwati for her entertainment. The second and remaining sixteen books contain adventures, tales, stories, and narratives of many kinds and descriptions, running one into the other.

A complete translation of this book would be interesting, and doubtless many of the stories would be found to tally with those forming portions of the Arabic, Persian, and European groups. Whether the substance of them came from the East to the West, or whether the stories came spontaneously to the brain of each author, it is difficult to say. Anyhow an analogy does exist, and the best solution is that each author produced two kinds of tales, those which he had heard or read before, or which had come under his own experience; and those which sprang from his own brain, and came to the surface of their own accord, like Venus rising from the sea, a thing of beauty and of joy for ever.

"The Kathásaritságara," Wilson writes, "is full of interest as abounding with pictures of national manners and feelings, and as offering the oldest extant form of many of the tales which were once popular in Europe. They show plainly enough that the Hindoos occupy an early and a prominent place in the history of fiction."

As a complete analysis of the whole work would occupy too much space, three stories are given to serve as specimens of Hindoo humour.

THE MAID, THE MONKEY, AND THE MENDICANT.

On the banks of the Ganges there was once a city named Makandi. And in a temple, not far from the river, there lived a religious mendicant with a large number of disciples. He was a great rogue, but to impress the minds of the credulous people of the neighbourhood, he affected to be perfectly indifferent to all worldly affairs, and even went so far as to have taken a vow of perpetual silence. Now, in this city there resided a wealthy merchant, who believed in the mendicant, and was one of his devoted followers. The merchant had a beautiful daughter, who had just come of age, and who, entertaining a tender feeling for a handsome prince who lived in the neighbourhood, had begun to communicate with him by means of a confidential servant. One day the mendicant came on a begging excursion to the house of the merchant, and his daughter, beautifully dressed, came out with a silver cup in her hand to give him alms. The beggar as soon as he saw her forgot his vow of perpetual silence, and exclaimed, "Oh! what a sight!" but immediately afterwards he was ashamed of the words which he had uttered, and hastened home to the temple. The merchant, who had heard these words, thought that there was something unusual in them, and followed the mendicant to his abode. The latter, on seeing him, said with tears in his eyes, "Friend, I know that you are greatly devoted to me, and I grieve to say that a great misfortune will come upon you. The marks upon the body of your beautiful daughter foretell the ruin of your family, and the loss of your wealth as soon as she is married." These words frightened the merchant almost out of his wits, and he implored the hypocritical mendicant to tell him if there were any means of averting the catastrophe. "There is one remedy," he replied, "but you will find it hard to practise. You must make a box with holes in the lid, in the form of a boat, and having administered a narcotic to your daughter, place her in it, and closing the box, put it into the Ganges with a lamp burning on it. The waters of the river will carry her to some distant country, where doubtless she will be married, but her marriage there will not affect your fortune here." Pleased with this apparently disinterested advice, the silly merchant returned home, and did as he was told. Fortunately, however, for the girl, her confidential servant heard what was going to be done, and immediately informed the young prince, the girl's lover, of the intentions of her father. At night he accordingly watched by the river, and as soon as the box was left there he got hold of it, and brought it home, and taking the sleeping girl out, put in to her place a large and ferocious monkey, and, having closed the lid, sent it back to the river upon whose broad stream it was floated once more. In the meantime the mendicant was enjoying golden dreams about the future. Thinking to secure the girl for himself, he sent some of his disciples to the river side, and told them to get hold of the box as it came floating down the stream. He further enjoined them not to pay any attention to anything they might hear inside the box, but to bring it directly to him as soon as they found it. On the box being brought, he had it carried to his cell, and then told his disciples to remain at a distance, and not to disturb him, as he had to perform some religious ceremonies in connection with it. The disciples then retired, and the mendicant began to open the box with the most pleasing anticipations. But alas, the retribution of sin is often too near. The ferocious monkey, exasperated by his confinement, jumped out at once, and began to bite, scratch, and tear the poor mendicant in every way. The latter bawled out as loud as he could, but his disciples thinking that he was performing religious ceremonies, or fighting with the devil, did not come to his assistance. At last he succeeded in opening the door of his room, and got away with the loss of his nose and an ear. The monkey also bolted through the door, and disappeared into the jungle. The good people of Nakandi were much amused with the incident, and drove the mendicant out of the town. The merchant's daughter was delighted to find herself with her lover, while her father, covered with shame, consoled himself with the idea that she had got a good husband.

THE BRAHMAN'S REVENGE.

In the city of Mathura there once lived a famous dancing-girl named Rupinika. She had an old adopted mother, who had trained her up in all the arts necessary for carrying out her profession. Now, it happened one day that Rupinika went to visit a temple, and there met a poor young handsome Brahman named Lohajangha. Instantly falling in love with him, she brought him to her abode, and thenceforth began to serve him as her husband, to the exclusion of every other person. Her mother was naturally enraged at this strange conduct, so unbecoming a dancing-girl, but not being able to dissuade her by simple remonstrances, she had recourse to a stratagem. One morning, a prince with a large number of followers happened to pass by her door, so she asked him to drive away the useless man from her house, and take possession of her daughter. The prince ordered his followers to seize Lohajangha, and to throw him into a dirty pit, and then went on his way without caring further about Rupinika.

Covered with shame and grief, the poor Brahman got out of the ditch, and resolving to remain no longer in that city, he started to travel so as to forget his grief. One day, while crossing a river, he was carried away by the current to the sea. By the aid of a plank he kept himself above water, until by the force of the wind he was carried to Ceylon. On his arrival in the island, the demons at once brought the circumstance to the notice of their king, Bibhishana, who, knowing the power of human beings by reason of the conquest of his island by Rama, caused the Brahman to be brought with great respect to his palace, and presented him with a large quantity of gold. He also gave him a large eagle for his conveyance, and at the time of his departure sent with him the four weapons* of the

* These are the Chakra or wheel, the club or mace, the conch shell, and the lotus, and are known in Hindu mythology as the four weapons or arms in the hands of Vishnu.

god Vishnu, all made of gold, to be presented to the temple of that god at Mathura. On his arrival there, Lohajangha took up his abode in an old lonely temple outside the town, and began to think how he was to punish the vile mother of Rupinika for her behaviour towards himself. He therefore mounted his eagle, and wearing on his body all the weapons of Vishnu which he had brought for the temple, he went at night to the house of Rupinika, and awakening her, announced himself as the god Vishnu, who had come to favour her on account of her many virtues. The dancing-girl was overjoyed at the idea of having fetched a deity, and attracted the heart of a god, and after feeling the actual touch of his body considered that she was no longer a mortal. The next day she would hardly speak to her mother, and with great difficulty was prevailed upon to relate what had occurred on the previous night. The mother was not less credulous than the daughter, but after hearing Rupinika's story, and seeing Lohajangha herself the next night, she was so thoroughly convinced of his godhead, that on the third day she requested her daughter to try and bring about her admission into the blessed region of heaven before her death. The dancing-girl promised to do what she could, and at night implored her lover, on behalf of her mother, to grant the request. In reply, he said that it would be impossible on ordinary days, but that the gates of heaven were left open on the eleventh day in each fortnight, so that the followers of Shiva might enter the heavenly regions. With them she might be introduced if she would take their form, which is this: "She must shave her head, preserving five locks upon it. On her neck she must wear a garland of human skulls. One-half of her face must be painted black, and the other half red. And last of all, she must appear entirely naked. If she assumes this form, I can undertake to carry her to heaven." The daughter conveyed this message carefully to her mother, who felt excessively delighted, and carried out her preparations to the letter. At the appointed hour on the eleventh day of the fortnight, our human god took the wretch before him on his eagle, and sitting her on the top of a lofty pillar near the temple of Vishnu outside the city, he told her to wait for him there. With a loud voice from above, he then warned the people that a destructive plague was about to fall upon them, and that they should therefore assemble at once at the temple of Vishnu, and pray for their safety. The populace obeyed this heavenly voice, and assembled in large numbers near the temple. Lohajangha then changed his dress and joined the crowd. In the meanwhile the unfortunate woman, unable to remain any longer standing on the pillar, cried out most piteously to the assembled crowd, "Oh! I fall down—I fall down." These words created additional fear in the minds of the people, who thought that it was the deity of the plague who threatened them with her fall. The people therefore prayed to her with all their might not to fall until the next morning. This lasted all night. At the dawn of day the people recognized the old woman of their city on the top of the pillar, and took her down. She then told them her story, which was heard with astonishment, and the king of the place offered a reward to any person who would explain the matter. Lohajangha then came forward, and relating his adventures, presented the weapons in gold for the use of the temple of Vishnu. The king was amused and pleased, and ordered Rupinika to be handed over to Lohajangha as a reward for all that he had gone through on her behalf.

THE MIRROR.

In the wealthy city of Pataliputra, the modern Patna, there once lived a Brahman named Rudra-surman. He had a wife called Gunevati, who died ten days after giving birth to a male child. The father of the child was therefore obliged to bring him up by the hands of a nurse. As it is natural that no child thrives so well under a nurse as under the tender care of a mother, the boy did not grow up well. He had thin arms and legs and a big pot-like belly, and when he was ten years old, he looked like a boy of six. As is often the case with boys of such peculiar physiognomy, there was a great deal of cunning and rascality in his character. And from his curious figure his father called him by the name of Tundila.

Some time after the death of Gunevati, the mother of this boy, his father married another girl named Lalita. The girl was beautiful, but at the same time unchaste. There can be no real love between a young wife and an old husband, and such was the case with Lalita, who fell desperately in love with a young and good-looking Brahman named Guvadatta. Now Rudra-surman was in the service of the king of that place, and whenever he was absent from his house on duty, Guvadatta used to come there to see the wife, and made himself very agreeable. This was known to the cunning boy Tundila, but as his stepmother was very kind to him and gave him good food and clothes, he used to assist her in all these things, instead of annoying her in any way. He made himself very useful also in conveying messages, and watching at the door of the house.

Now, it happened one day that Tundila was annoyed with his stepmother on account of her not giving him what he wanted, so he determined to raise some suspicion in his father's mind about her conduct. One day when his father came home he began to jump about, and striking the palms of his hands together, shouted out, "I have two papas, I have two papas;" "one comes from this road, and the other comes from that road." On hearing these words Rudra-surman was startled, and thought to himself, what is the boy saying, and what does he mean? He then called the boy to him, and asked him what he meant. The boy remained quite silent, and when his father pressed him for an answer he burst into tears. This circumstance made Rudra-surman very suspicious about his wife, and a man who once becomes suspicious is always anxious and always thinking about her conduct, and making guesses to her disadvantage. And this was the case with Rudra-surman. He could not procure any definite information from his son, yet his mind began to wander in the ocean of suspicion. Sometimes he allowed his mind to be dragged into the waves of the idea of his wife's unchastity, and at other times he was floating quietly on the still waves of the idea of her innocence.

Owing to the constant fluctuations of his mind, he ceased to talk and chatter with his wife as usual, and somehow or other always took offence at every little thing that she did. By this change in his conduct towards her, his wife understood that there was something wrong, and she rightly imagined that it must be the result of Tundila's mischief, especially as she was aware that she had annoyed him some days previously. After considering for some time, one day, during the absence of her husband at the court, she called Tundila to her, and pleased him much by giving him some good food and clothes. After this, she said to him, "My dear Tundila, I love you more than my own eyes, and I shall give you everything you want without telling your father about it. You know how stingy he is, and how he never gives you anything, but how readily I supply everything that you want. Look here, I have bought this ivory toy elephant for you; take it, and amuse yourself with it." Women, by their sweet speech and insinuating manners, can pacify all kinds of men. What difficulty can they experience in coaxing a little boy? Tundila was much pleased, and said, "Mamma, I love you better than my papa, and I shall always be obedient to you."

Lalita: My darling child, now tell me whether you said anything about me to your papa?

Tundila: One day that you did not give me anything to eat, I was very angry with you, and that day I raised some suspicion in his mind about you, by saying, "I have two papas." I have, however, said nothing more than that.

Lalita: Did you really only say that much?

Tundila: By God, I never tell lies.

Lalita: Never mind, then, but do as I tell you. Act just in the same manner as you did before; but look at the mirror that is fixed on the wall yonder, and shout, "I have two papas, I have two papas; one comes from within the mirror, and the other from outside."

Tundila agreed to do this; and when Rudra-surman entered the house, the boy acted accordingly. Directly Rudra-surman heard the words, his suspicions all vanished, and he began to reproach himself, saying, "What a great mistake I have made; from the former words of the boy, I falsely suspected my pure and innocent wife."

CHAPTER IV.

THE DUSA-KUMARA-CHARITA, OR THE ADVENTURES OF THE TEN YOUTHS OR PRINCES.

COLEBROOKE has given the Hitopodesa the first place in his collection of Sanscrit works prepared for the use of students. The second place, however, he allotted to the Dusa-kumara-charita, or adventures of the ten youths or princes, which he abridged from the celebrated poem of Dandi, supposed to have been written about the end of the eleventh century. This distinguished poet, he says, was famous above all other bards for the sweetness of his language, and composed this pleasing story in harmonious verse. It is divided into two parts, the first containing five chapters, the other eight. The first part ends with the marriage of the principal hero, the other contains the adventures of the same prince and his companions. About them P. W. Jacob, whose translation has been chiefly adopted, says: "Some of the incidents correspond with those of the Arabian nights, but the stories on the whole are quite different from anything found there, and give a lively picture of Hindoo manners and morals. Unscrupulous deception, ready invention, extreme credulity and superstition, and disregard of human life are strongly illustrated." Belief in the power of penance is often alluded to, as also the transmigration of souls, and the agency of supernatural beings. Space will only permit a brief analysis of the work, and the adventures of one of the youths.

In Pushpapuri, a city of Magadha, ruled Rajahansa, a great king. His queen's name was Vasumati. He had three ministers, of whom No. 1 had three sons, who for brevity can be called A, B, and C; No. 2 had two sons, D and E; and No. 3 also two, F and G. Now, G became disgusted with the world, and started on a pilgrimage to foreign lands. C attached himself to low company, parasites, actors, and women, and led a vagabond life, while E was constantly travelling on mercantile business. The other four, A, B, D, and F, succeeded to the ministerial situations held by their fathers.

Now, it happened that a great war broke out between Rajahansa, king of Magadha, and Manasara, king of Malava, in which the latter was totally defeated, but was immediately restored to his liberty and his kingdom by the former. Subsequently another war took place, with the opposite result, and Manasara, the conqueror on this occasion, took possession of Rajahansa's country, while Rajahansa himself, having been left for dead in his chariot, was carried off by the horses uncontrolled into the jungles, where he was found by the queen. With the aid of her attendants she brought the king to life again, and they then both went into exile.

Shortly after the Queen Vasumati gave birth to a young prince named (1) Rajavahana, and the four ministers, A, B, D, and F, also each had a son named (2) Mitrogupta, (3) Mantragupta, (4) Visruta, and (5) Pramati respectively. They all grew up together as the playfellows and friends of the prince Rajavahana, five in all. This is followed by the tales connected with the loss and recovery of (6) Upaharavarna, and (7) Apaharavarma, the twin sons of the Prince of Mithila, an ally of the king Rajahansa, also of E's son named (8) Pusbadhana, of C's son named (9) Arthapala, and of G's son named (10) Somadatta. Thus it happened that these ten boys were brought up and educated together, and taught to write and speak various tongues, as also the holy sciences, policy, rhetoric, history and the sacred records, metaphysics, astrology, law, the morals of princes, the science of music, medicine and magic, playing on instruments, how to manage the horse, elephant and car, the use of arms, and how to excel in thieving, gaming, and other such practices. The king, seeing their youth, skill, and vigour, was proud of his juvenile band, and felt confident of triumphing with their aid over every danger.

The time then came that the young Prince Rajahavana had to start on his travels along with the other nine youths to see the world and gain experience. After their arrival in the Vindya forest the Prince got separated from his companions, and did not return, having gone off into the forest with a Brahman named Metanga, that he met there. The nine youths searched for him in vain, and then agreed to separate, and to look for him individually, and after prosecuting their inquiries for some time to meet again finally at Ujjayini.

The adventures of the Prince, the story of his marriage, and the tale of the wanderings of each of his companions, are then given separately, as they by degrees meet each other again, or are curiously brought together. The stories are all more or less amusing, but space will only allow one to be given, viz.,

THE ADVENTURES OF (7) APAHARAVARMA, RELATED BY HIMSELF TO THE PRINCE AS FOLLOWS:

My lord, when you had gone away with the Brahman, and we were unable to find you, I wandered about searching for you like the rest of your friends. One day I heard by chance of a very famous Muni or holy man devoted to study, meditation, and penance, living in a forest on the banks of the Ganges not far from Champa, and who was said to have supernatural knowledge of past and future events. Hoping to obtain some information about you, I determined to seek him out, and accordingly came here for that purpose. Having found the way to his dwelling, I saw there a miserable-looking man, very unlike the holy devotee whom I had pictured to myself. Sitting down, however, beside this person, I said, "I have come a long way to consult the celebrated Rishi (or holy man retired from the world and devoted to prayer and meditation) Marichi, having heard that he is possessed of very wonderful knowledge. Can you tell me where to find him?"

Deeply sighing, he answered: "There was not long ago such a person in this place, but he is changed; he is no longer what he was." "How can that be?" I asked. "One day," he replied, "while that Muni was engaged in prayer and meditation, he was interrupted by the sudden arrival of a famous actress and dancer, called Kamamanjari, who, with dishevelled hair and eyes full of tears, threw herself at his feet. Before he had time to ask the meaning of this, a confused crowd of her companions came up, headed by an old woman, the mother of Kamamanjari, apparently in great agitation and distress. When they were all a little quieted, he asked the girl the meaning of her tears, and for what purpose she had come to him.

She answered, apparently with great respect and bashfulness, "O reverend sir, I have heard of your great wisdom and your kindness to those who are willing to give up the pleasures of this world for the sake of the next. I am tired of the disgraceful life I am leading, and wish to renounce it." Upon this, her mother, with her loose grey hairs touching the ground, interrupted her and said, "Worthy sir, this daughter of mine would make it appear that I am to blame, but, indeed, I have done my duty, and have carefully prepared her for that profession for which, by birth, she was intended. From earliest childhood I have bestowed the greatest care upon her, doing everything in my power to promote her health and beauty. As soon as she was old enough, I had her carefully instructed in the arts of dancing, acting, playing on musical instruments, singing, painting, preparing perfumes and flowers, in writing and conversation, and even to some extent in grammar, logic, and philosophy. She was taught to play various games with skill and dexterity, how to dress well, and show herself off to the greatest advantage in public; I hired persons to go about praising her skill and her beauty, and to applaud her when she performed in public, and I did many other things to promote her success, and to secure for her liberal remuneration; yet after all the time, trouble, and money which I have spent upon her, just when I was beginning to reap the fruit of my labours, the ungrateful girl has fallen in love with a stranger, a young Brahman, without property, and wishes to marry him and give up her profession, notwithstanding all my entreaties and representations of the poverty and distress to which all her family will be reduced if she persists in her purpose; and because I oppose this marriage, she declares that she will renounce the world and become a devotee."

The Muni compassionately said to the girl, "You will never be able to endure the hardships of such a life as you propose to lead, a life so different from that to which you have been accustomed. A life of devotion is a life of suffering. Its object is either absorption or paradise; the first is only to be reached by the perfection of wisdom, a thing not easily effected; but heaven may be attained by all who duly perform the duties of their station. Take my advice, then; give up all thoughts of an undertaking which you will never accomplish, comply with your mother's wishes, return with her, and be content with that way of life in which you have been brought up."

With many tears she replied, "If you will not receive me I will put an end to my wretched life."

Finding her so determined, the Muni, after some reflection, said to the mother and her companions, "Go away for the present, and come back after a few days. I will give her good advice, and you will, no doubt, find her tired of living here, and quite ready to return." Thereupon they all went away, and she was left alone with the Muni. At first she kept at a distance from him, taking care not to interrupt him in his meditations, but waiting on him unobtrusively, rendering him many little services, watering his favourite trees, and gathering sacred grass and flowers for offering to the gods. Then, as he became more accustomed to her, she would amuse him with songs and dances, and at last began to sit near him, and talk of the pleasures of love.

One day, as if in all simplicity, she said, "Surely people are very wrong in reckoning virtue, wealth, and pleasure as the three great objects of life."

"Tell me," he answered, "how far do you regard virtue as superior to the other two?"

"A very wise man like you," she replied, "can hardly learn anything from an ignorant woman like me; but, since you ask, I will tell you what I think. There is no real acquisition of happiness or wealth without virtue, but the latter is quite independent of the other two. Without it a man is nothing; but if he fully possesses it, he is so purified by it that he may indulge in pleasures occasionally, and any sin connected with them will no more adhere to him than dust to a cloud. Look at all the stories of the amours of the gods. Are they the less worshipped on that account? I think, therefore, that virtue is a hundred times superior to the other two." With many such specious arguments as these, and by her winning ways, she contrived to make him madly in love; so that, forgetting all his religious duties and former austerities, he thought only how to please her.

When she perceived this, she said to him, "Let us stay no longer in the forest, but go to my house in the town, where we can have many more enjoyments." Utterly infatuated, he was ready to do her bidding, and she, having procured a covered carriage, took him in the evening to her own house. The next day there was a great festival, at which the king was accustomed to appear in public and converse familiarly with his subjects. On such occasions he would often be surrounded by actresses and dancing-girls.

On that day Kamamanjari persuaded the Muni to put on a gay dress, and accompany her to the park where the festival was held; and he, thinking only of her, and miserable if she were away from him even for a short time, consented to go. On their arrival there she walked with him towards the king, who, seeing her, said with a smile, "Sit down here with that reverend man," and all eyes were directed towards him.

Presently one of the ladies rose up, and making a low obeisance to the king, said, "My lord, I must confess myself beaten by that lady. I have lost my wager, and must now pay the penalty." Then a great shout of laughter arose, the king congratulated Kamamanjari, and presented her with handsome ornaments.

After this she walked away with the astonished Muni, followed by a great crowd, shouting applause. Before reaching her own house, she turned round to him with a low obeisance, and said, "Reverend sir, you have favoured me with your company a long time; it will be well for you to attend now to your own affairs." Not having his eyes yet opened, he started as if thunderstruck, and said, "My dear, what does all this mean? what has become of the great love which you professed for me?" She smilingly answered, "I will explain it all. One day that lady whom you saw in the park had a dispute with me as to which was the most attractive. At last she said, 'You boast of your powers, forsooth; go and try them on Marichi. If you can persuade him to accompany you here, then indeed you may triumph. I will acknowledge myself your inferior.' This was the reason of my coming to you; the trick has been successful; I have won my wager, and have no further occasion for you."

Bowed down by shame and remorse, the unhappy man slunk back to his hermitage, miserable and degraded, bitterly lamenting his folly and infatuation, but resolved to atone for it by deep repentance and severe penance.

"I am that wretched man: you see, therefore, that I am now quite unable to assist you. But do not go away, remain in Champa; after a time I shall recover my former power." While he was telling me this sad story, the sun set, and I remained with him that night. The next morning at sunrise, I took leave of him, and walked towards the city. On my way thither, as I passed a Buddhist monastery, I was struck by the appearance of a man sitting at the side of the road near it. He was extraordinarily ugly, his body naked, with the exception of a rag round his waist, and his face so covered with dirt, that the tears he was shedding left furrows as they rolled down his cheeks. Moved by compassion, I sat down near him, and inquired the reason of his distress, at the same time adding, "If it is a secret, I do not wish to intrude upon you." "My misfortunes are well known," he answered; "I can have no objection to telling you, if you wish to hear them." Then he began: "My name is Vasupalika, but, from my ugliness, I am generally known as Virupaka the deformed. I am the son of a man of some importance here, who left me a large fortune.

"Among my acquaintances there was a person called Sundaraka, remarkably handsome, but poor. Between us two some mischievous persons strove to excite a rivalry, pitting my money against his beauty and accomplishments. One day, in a large assembly, having got up a dispute between us, they said, 'It is not beauty or wealth, but the approbation of the ladies which stamps the worth of a man; therefore let the famous actress, Kamamanjari, decide between you, and agree that she shall say who is the best man.' To this we both assented; and she, having been previously prepared for the part which she was to perform, was brought into the room, and, passing by my rival with scorn, sat down by my side, and taking a garland from her own head placed it on mine.

"Greatly flattered and delighted by this preference, and blinded by a mad love for her which I had not ventured to express, I most readily gave myself up to her seductions, and in a very short time she obtained such an influence over me that everything I possessed was at her disposal. Before long, she had so plundered me, and led me into such extravagance, that I was reduced to the most abject poverty, and had nothing I could call my own but this miserable rag which you now see me wear.

"Cast off by her, blamed and reproached by the elder men, laughed at and despised by those who had been my companions in prosperity, I knew not where to turn, and, as a last resource, I entered this Buddhist monastery, where I obtain a bare subsistence. Distressed by the cutting off my long hair and by numerous restrictions as to eating, drinking, and sleeping, like a newly-caught elephant, and hearing every day abuse of those gods whom I used to worship, and filled with remorse for my departure from the religion of my ancestors, I am utterly miserable and only wish for death."

Having heard this pitiable story, I did what I could to comfort him, and said, "Do not despair; I have heard already of that wicked woman, and think I shall be able to find some means of making her restore to you a part at least of your property." After leaving him I went into the city, and finding, from popular report, that it was full of rich misers, I resolved to bring them to their proper condition by taking away their useless wealth.

Occupied by this thought I went into a gaming-house where I was much interested and amused by watching the players and observing their tricks, their sleight-of-hand, their bullying or cringing behaviour to each other; the reckless profusion of the winners, the muttering despair of those who had lost.

While overlooking a game of chess, I smiled and made some remark about a bad move of one of the players, upon which his opponent, turning to me with a sneer, said, "No doubt, you think yourself very clever, but wait till I have finished off this stupid fellow, and I will play you for any stake you like."

When the game was over, accepting his challenge, I sat down to play, and won altogether sixteen thousand dinars. Half of this sum I kept for myself, and the other half I divided between the gaming-house keeper and the players who were present. The latter were loud in praise of my generosity, and of the skill which I had shown in beating that boaster. The former asked me to dine with him, and I often went to his house, and became very intimate with him, and obtained from him much information, especially such as had reference to my purpose.

One very dark night, fully directed by him, I set out determined on robbery, and equipped with a dark dress, a short sword, a spade, a crowbar, a pair of pincers, a wooden man's head (to be pushed in through any opening in a wall, so as to receive any blow which might be given), a magic candle, a rope and grappling iron, a box with a bee in it (to be let loose that it might put out the lights), and other implements. Selecting a house where I knew there was much money, I made a hole in the wall, and finding all quiet, enlarged it, entered boldly, and carried off much booty.

As I was returning, and looking cautiously about me, I came suddenly upon a young woman, who was much alarmed at seeing me. Perceiving her agitation, I spoke to her kindly, and assured her that I would much rather assist her than injure her. Encouraged by my words, she told me her story: "My name is Kulapalika; I am the daughter of a rich merchant in this city, and was from childhood engaged to the son of another rich man named Dhanamittra; he, however, being of a very generous disposition, when he had succeeded to his father's property, was preyed on by pretended friends and reduced to comparative poverty. Seeing this my father refused his consent to our marriage, and in spite of my reluctance is determined to give me to a rich man called Arthapati. To escape this marriage I have slipped out from home by a secret passage, rarely used, and am going to the house of my lover, who is expecting me, and who will take me away to some other country; pray, do not detain me, but accept this." So saying, she put one of her ornaments into my hand; I did not refuse it, but walked by her side, intending to escort her to her destination. We had, however, only gone a few steps when I saw coming towards us, at no great distance, a large body of the citizen guard. Without losing a moment, I said to the trembling girl, "Don't be alarmed; say that I have been bitten by a serpent, and I will manage the rest."

By the time they had reached us I had thrown myself on the ground, and lay as if insensible, and she stood over me crying. On being questioned, she answered with many tears and in evident distress, "My husband and I, coming from the country, lost our way, and have only lately entered the city. Just now he was bitten by a serpent, and is all but dead. Is there any one among you skilled in charms who can recover him?"

Among the guards there chanced to be a very conceited man, who had often boasted of his skill, and was now delighted to have an opportunity of displaying it. He stood over me while the others waited, and with many gesticulations, muttered various charms, supposed to be efficacious in such a case, but finding all of no avail, said at last, "Ah!

it is too late, the poor man is past all remedies; what a pity I did not see him sooner." Then joining his companions, who were impatient to be off, he turned to the sobbing girl, and said, "He was evidently fated to die; who can prevail over fate? It is useless to lament; nothing more can be done now. Wait a little while, and when we come back we will remove the body."

As soon as they were out of sight, I rose up and took her to the house of Dhanamittra, and said to him, "I met this lady just now; I have brought her safely here, and now restore the ornament which she gave me in her fright, for, though I am a robber, I would not steal from one like her." Delighted at seeing her, he answered "Oh, sir, you have indeed rendered me a great service in bringing this dear one in safety here; such conduct is very extraordinary in a man of your way of life, and I am quite unable to understand your motives for acting thus. At all events I am under very great obligations to you, and command my services in future."

After some further talk I asked him, "Friend, what do you now intend to do?" "It will be impossible," he answered, "for me to live here if I marry her without her father's consent. I propose, therefore, to leave the town with her this very night." "A clever man," I replied, "is at home in any place. Wherever he goes, he may say, this is my country. But in travelling many hardships must be endured—hunger, thirst, fatigue, and dangers from men and wild beasts. How will this tender girl be able to bear them?

"You seem to be wanting in wisdom and forethought in thus abandoning home and country. Take courage, be guided by me, and you shall marry her and live comfortably here. But first we must take her back to her father's house."

To this he consented without hesitation, and we set out at once. Guided by her, we entered through the secret passage, and having left her at home, we carried off everything of value, and got away without exciting alarm.

Having hidden our booty in some old ruins close by, we were going home, when we fell in with some of the city guard. Fortunately there chanced to be an elephant tied up at the side of the road. We quickly, therefore, unfastened the rope, mounted him, and urged him at full speed, and before the watchmen could recover from their confusion were out of sight. Halting the elephant close to the wall of a deserted garden, we got over it with the help of the trees growing there, escaped on the other side, and reached home undetected. We then bathed and went to bed.

The next day we walked out carefully dressed, and were amused at hearing an exaggerated account of our adventures of the preceding night, which had caused much alarm and excitement in the city.

I had hoped by robbing the old man to prevent the marriage of his daughter with Arthapati. But this hope was frustrated, for the latter was not only willing to take Kulapalika without a dowry, but even made presents to her father, and it was settled that the marriage should take place at the end of a month. Finding this to be the case, I felt that something more must be done; and having hit upon a plan which I thought would be effectual, I gave Dhanamittra directions how to act.

Accordingly, a few days afterwards he went to the king, to whom he was previously known, and having asked for a private audience, said, "A very wonderful thing has happened to me, of which it seems right that your majesty should be informed. You have known me as Dhanamittra, the son of a very rich man. During my prosperity I was engaged to the daughter of a wealthy merchant, but when I was reduced to poverty, he refused his consent to our marriage, and is now about to give her to another.

"Driven to despair by the double loss of fortune and wife, I went into a wood near the city, intending to put an end to my wretched life. There, when in the act of cutting my throat, I was stopped by a very aged devotee, who asked the cause of the rash act.

"'Poverty and contempt,' I answered.

"'There is nothing more foolish and sinful than suicide,' he replied. 'A man of sense will endure adversity rather than escape from it in such a manner. Wealth, when lost, may be regained in many ways, but life in none. A broken fortune may be repaired; a cut throat can never be joined again. But why should I preach to you thus? Here is a remedy for your misfortunes. This leather bag will give you abundant wealth. I have used it for assisting the deserving, but now I am old and infirm, and am not long for this world. I give it to you. Go home; if you possess anything wrongfully acquired, restore it to the rightful owner, and give away the rest of your property to Brahmans and the poor. When this has been done, put away the purse carefully, and in the morning it will be found full of gold. Remember that whoever possesses it must comply with these conditions, and that it will yield its treasures only to a merchant like yourself or to an actress.'

"With these words he handed me the purse, and immediately disappeared.

"I have now brought the purse to your majesty, to know your pleasure concerning it."

The king, though much astonished, believed the

story, and told him to keep it and enjoy it; and, in answer to his entreaty, promised that any one attempting to steal it should be severely punished. After this, Dhanamittra, making no secret of his acquisition of the purse, disposed of all his property somewhat ostentatiously, leaving himself absolutely nothing but the clothes which he wore; and in the morning having filled the purse with gold, the proceeds of the robbery, he showed it to his neighbours, who were fully convinced of its magic powers.

The fame of the purse was thus spread abroad, and we were able to account for our newly-acquired wealth without incurring any suspicion as to the manner of obtaining it.

At this time, for reasons which will presently appear, I induced one Vimardaka to enter the service of Arthapati, and directed him to use all possible means to excite his master against Dhanamittra. In this he had no difficulty; for the father of Kulapalika, hearing of Dhanamittra's sudden acquisition of wealth, did not even wait to be asked, but of his own accord renewed the former engagement and rejected Arthapati.

About that time it was publicly announced that a younger sister of Kamamanjari—Ragamanjari by name—would make her first appearance as a dancer and singer. Great expectations having been raised, a large number of spectators, including myself and my friend Dhanamittra, were present at the performance.

I was struck with her beauty the instant she appeared on the stage; but when I heard her sweet voice, and saw her graceful movements, I was perfectly enchanted, and unable to take my eyes off her for a moment.

The performance ended, she withdrew, followed

by the longing eyes and loud applause of the spectators, and giving, as I fancied, a significant look at me. The next day I was anxious, restless, and unable to eat, and could do nothing but roam about listlessly, or lie on the couch, thinking of her, and making the excuse of a bad headache. My friend seeing me in this state, easily guessed the reason of it, and said to me in private, "I know the cause of your uneasiness, and can give you good hopes." That girl is virtuous, whatever her mother and sister may be; and having watched her closely at the performance, I am convinced that she was much struck with you; therefore if you are willing to make her your wife, there will be no great difficulties to overcome as far as she is concerned; for resisting all seductions and the persuasions of her wicked mother and sister, she has declared, "No man shall have me except as a wife, and I must be won by merit, not by money." On the other hand, her mother and sister, fearing lest she should be withdrawn from the stage, have gone to the king, and obtained, by means of many tears and entreaties, a decree that if any man shall take the girl, either in marriage or not, without her mother's consent, he shall be put to death like a robber. Therefore, when you have gained her love, you must also obtain the mother's consent, and that can only be done by means of a large bribe; she will not listen to any other inducement." "I am equal to all this," I answered. "I will win the young lady, and find means to satisfy the old one." And I lost no time in accomplishing my purpose. It was first necessary to make acquaintance with Kamamanjari, and to this end I found out a woman often employed by her as a messenger, and having gained her over by bribes, sent through her a number of small presents, till at last, Kamamanjari was disposed in my favour, and received me at her house. Meanwhile I contrived to have secret interviews with her beautiful sister, who consented to become my wife. As soon as this was settled, I said to Kamamanjari, "I am desirous of obtaining your mother's consent to my marriage with your sister, who has accepted me. I know that if she ceases to perform you will lose a large income, and therefore offer you in return something better, and more certain. Procure for me the desired permission, and you shall have Dhanamittra's magic purse, which I will safely steal for you."

Delighted at the prospect of possessing inexhaustible wealth, she agreed to the proposal; the mother's consent was formally given, and on the day of my marriage, I secretly handed over the promised purse.

Very soon after, Vimardaka, by my directions in a large assembly, began to abuse and insult Dhanamittra, who, as if much astonished, said, "What does all this mean? Why should you annoy me? I am not aware that I have ever given you offence."

He answered furiously, "You purse-proud wretch, do you think I will not take my master Arthapati's part? Have you not robbed him of his intended wife by bribing her father? Do you think he has no cause for anger against you? His interests are mine; I am ready to risk my life for him, and I will pay you off. Some day you shall miss that purse, the source of the riches with which you are so puffed up." Saying this, he rushed out of the place in a rage, and though nothing was done at the time, his words were not forgotten.

Then Dhanamittra went to the king, and declaring that he had lost the purse, mentioned his suspicion of Arthapati, and the reason for it. He, having heard nothing of what his servant had said, when summoned and asked, "Have you a confidential servant named Vimardaka?" answered, without hesitation, "Certainly; he is a very trustworthy man, and entirely devoted to my interest." "Then bring him here," was the reply. Thus commanded, he searched everywhere for his servant, but was unable to find him, and for a good reason, for I had furnished the man with money, and sent him to Oojein to look for you—*i.e.*, for the prince Rajahavana. The supposed thief having disappeared, his master was put in prison till further evidence could be procured, for no one but those in the secret doubted that he was the instigator of the theft.

Meanwhile, Kamamanjari, anxious to make use of the magic purse, proceeded to fulfil the conditions attached to its use. She went secretly to Virupaka, the deformed one, and restored the money of which she had robbed him, and then gave away all her furniture, clothes, and ornaments. This, however, she did so incautiously that attention was drawn to it; upon which Dhanamittra went again to the king, saying, "I suspect that the actress Kamamanjari has got my purse, for though notoriously avaricious, she is giving away everything she possesses, and there must be some strong reason for such a proceeding." In consequence of this information, she was summoned to appear the next day, together with her mother, and the two women came in great alarm to consult me.

I said to Kamamanjari, "No doubt, you are suspected of having the purse. This suspicion has arisen from your own imprudence in giving away your property so openly. I much fear that you will have to give it up, and you will be fortunate if you escape without worse consequences. But you must on no account implicate me; for that I should be put to death, all my property would be confiscated, your sister would die of grief, and you would be utterly ruined."

She answered, with many tears, "It is indeed my own fault, but you shall be safe. That niggardly wretch Arthapati is known to be intimate with me. I will say that I received it from him, and as he is already suspected of stealing it, I shall probably be believed." To this I agreed, and the next day when questioned, she at first denied all knowledge of the purse, then admitted having received it, but refused to say from whom, and at last, when threatened with torture, confessed, apparently with great reluctance, that Arthapati was the giver, and this being considered sufficient evidence against him, he was condemned to death.

Then Dhanamittra interceded for him, saying, "A decree was formerly made by one of your ancestors that no merchant or trader should be put to death for theft. I humbly entreat, therefore, that his life may be spared." To this the king consented. The poor wretch was banished, and all his property confiscated, a portion of it being given to Kamamanjari at the earnest entreaty of Dhanamittra, who got back his purse, and shortly afterwards married Kulapalika.

Having thus performed the promise to my friend, I increased my own wealth, and kept up the reputation of the purse by going on with my robberies, and so impoverished the rich misers that some of them were glad to receive a morsel of food from the beggars to whom they had formerly refused help, and who were now enriched by my liberality.

Still no suspicion fell on me; but fate is all powerful, and it was decreed that I should be caught at last.

One night sitting with my charming wife, intoxicated partly with wine, and partly with her sweet caresses, I was seized with madness, and started up, saying, "All the wealth in the city is not too much for you, I will fill the house with jewels for your sake." Then, like a furious elephant who has broken his chain, I rushed out, in spite of her remonstrances, with a drawn sword, and attacked a body of police who happened to be passing. They shouting out, "This is the robber," soon overpowered me, and I fell to the ground.

The shock sobered me at once, and all the horror of the situation into which I had brought myself by my folly came into my mind. I thought to myself my intimacy with Dhanamittra is well known, suspicion will fall on him, and unless I can turn it off, he, as well as my wife, will be arrested to-morrow. I quickly formed a plan by which they, and, perhaps, I myself, might be saved. But no time was to be lost, and as they were about to take me away, I called out to my wife's nurse Sringalika, who had followed me, "Begone, old wretch! and tell that vile harlot, your mistress, and her paramour, Dhanamittra, that she will never see her ornaments, nor he his magic purse again. I care not for life, if I am revenged on those two wretches."

The old woman being remarkably quick-witted, at once understood my object in speaking thus, and very humbly accosting the police, said, "Worthy sir, I entreat you to wait a moment, while I ask your prisoner where he has hid the ornaments of my mistress." To this they assented; and, coming to me, she said, "Oh, sir, your jealousy is without cause; whatever attentions that man may have paid my mistress, she is not to blame. Now that you are taken from her, she will have no means of support, and must go on the stage again. How can she do this without her ornaments? Take compassion on her, and say where you have hid them."

Then as if my anger was appeased, I answered, "Why should I, who am about to die, harbour resentment? Come close, and I will whisper where I have put them." In this manner I managed to give her a few hurried instructions. She went away with many blessings on me, and thanks to the men for their kindness; and I was taken to the king's prison.

At that time the governor of the prison was a very conceited young man, named Kantaka, who had lately succeeded to the office by the death of his father. When I was brought in, looking at me in a very contemptuous manner, he said, "So you are the thief who has committed so many robberies. If you do not give up the stolen property, and especially the magic purse, you shall suffer every possible variety of torture before you are put to death."

I answered, smiling, "Even though I should give up all the other stolen property, I will never let the purse go back to that wretch, Dhanamittra, my greatest enemy. You may try all your tortures, you will never get this secret out of me." Finding the fear of torture to have no effect, the next day he tried promises, and so went on from day to day, with alternate soothing and threatening. Meanwhile my wounds were attended to, and I was well fed, so that I had regained my strength, when, one day, Sringalika made her appearance, well dressed, and with cheerful countenance. To my surprise, she was allowed to speak to me in private. She said to me joyfully, "Your plan has succeeded. As you directed, I went to Dhanamittra, and told him from you, 'You must go at once to the king, and say the magic purse so lately restored, has again been stolen by one whom I regarded as a friend, a certain gambler, the husband of the actress, Rajamanjara. He has taken it from spite, being jealous of his wife, to whom, from kindness, I often made presents. He is now in prison for other offences, and if he is put to death immediately, as he deserves, I fear that I shall never recover my purse. I pray, therefore, that he may not be executed before he has confessed where it is concealed. For he admits having taken it; but declares that he will not give it up unless his life is spared.' Your friend admiring your ingenuity, and having full confidence in your resources, immediately went to the king, and obtained his request, so that your life is safe for the present."

"Meanwhile, with the help of gifts furnished by my mistress, I have formed an intimacy with the nurse of the Princess Ambalika, and have been introduced by her to the princess, whose favour I have gained by telling her amusing stories, and whom I have induced to feel an interest in the misfortune of my mistress. One day, when I was standing near her in the gallery round the courtyard of the palace, Kantaka, the governor of the prison, having some business or other, passed through below us. Picking up a flower which the princess had dropped, I let it fall on his head, and when he looked up to see from whose hand it came, I managed to make the princess laugh at something which I said, and the conceited fool, thinking that it was she who had dropped it to attract his attention, went away looking quite pleased and confused.

"That same evening I received a present for my mistress—a small basket marked with the signet of the princess, and containing articles of no great value. This I took to Kantaka, and, begging him to observe the strictest secrecy, made him believe that the princess had sent it to him. He was even delighted when, another day, I bought him a dirty dress, telling him that she had worn it. Finding him quite ready to believe this, and convinced that she was in love with him, I kept up an imaginary correspondence, bringing very loving messages from her, which I invented, and receiving many from him in return, which I took care not to deliver. His presents, of course, I kept for myself.

"In this manner I have raised his hopes very high, and, to encourage him still further, I said, 'I have heard from a learned astrologer with whom I am acquainted that you have certain marks upon you which indicate that you will one day be a king. This love on the part of the princess tends to the fulfilment of the prediction. You are, therefore, on the high road to fortune. If you have spirit enough to pursue it, all you have to do now is to obtain a secret interview with the lady; the rest will follow in due time.'

"'But how can I manage this?' he asked. 'The wall of the garden,' I replied, 'communicating with the princess's apartment, is separated from those of the gaol by a space of a few yards only. You could not get over these walls, but you might make an underground passage and slip in unobserved, and I will take care that there shall be some one to receive and conduct you to the princess. When once with her you are safe, for all her attendants are attached to her; not one would betray the secret."

"'But how can I make this underground passage?' he asked. 'I cannot dig it myself, or employ workmen.'

"'Have you no clever thief here,' I replied, 'accustomed to such work?'

"'Well suggested,' he answered; 'I have just the right man.'

"'Who is he?' I said.

"'That man who has stolen the magic purse,' said he. 'If he will set to work with a good will, he will soon dig his way through.'

"'Very good,' I answered. 'You must persuade him by promising to let him go when the work is done. But it would never do for him to be in the secret; therefore, when he has finished, put on his fetters again, and report to the king that he is excessively obstinate; that you have tried all other means to make him confess, and that nothing remains but to put him to torture. No doubt, the king will give orders accordingly, and you can easily manage so to inflict it that he shall die under it. When he is dead your secret will be safe; you can visit the princess as often as you like, and, doubtless, in the end the king, rather than disgrace his daughter, will consent to your marriage, and, as he has no other child, will make you his successor.'

"With this proposal he was quite delighted, and has been treating you well that you may have strength for the work. He intends to ask you to begin to-night, and has sent me to persuade you, believing me to be devoted to his interests, and looking forward to some great reward when he has got his wish."

Having heard this from the old woman, I gave her great praise, and said, "Lose no time. Tell him I am quite ready to do the work."

After this, Kantaka came to me and told me what he wanted, and swore a solemn oath that I should be liberated when the work was done; and I, in return, swore to keep his secret. Then he took off my fetters, I got a bath and a good dinner, and presently set to work in a dark corner under the wall. Soon after midnight the work was done, and an opening made into the courtyard of the women's apartments. Before returning I thought to myself, "This man has sworn an oath which he intends to break; for the preservation, therefore, of my own life I shall be justified in killing him." Having formed this resolution, I went back to the prison where Kantaka was waiting for me. He told me it was necessary to replace my fetters for the present, and I appeared to acquiesce. But as he was stooping to fasten them I gave him a violent kick, and, before he could recover himself, I had snatched a short sword which he wore, and cut off his head. I then returned to Springalika, who had remained in the prison, and said to her, "I am not disposed to have had all this toil for nothing. Tell me the way into the ladies' rooms. I will go there, and steal something before I make my escape."

Having received her directions, I passed again through the tunnel which I had made, came up into the courtyard, and from thence entered a large lofty room lighted by jewelled lamps, where a number of women were sleeping.

There on a couch, ornamented with beautifully carved flowers, and resting on lion's feet, I saw the princess covered only by a thin silken petticoat, half sunk into a soft white feather bed, like lightning on an autumn cloud.

Fast asleep, as if wearied by much play, she lay in a very graceful attitude, with her delicate ankles crossed, her knees slightly drawn up; one lovely hand laid loosely on her side, the other beneath her head; her full bosom slowly heaved by gentle breathing, illuminated by the ruby necklace strung on burnished gold; the top-knot of her loosened hair hanging down like some graceful flower; her lips so bright that the opening of the mouth could hardly be distinguished, and her features, in calm repose, shaded by her lovely ringlets. I had entered so softly that no one was disturbed, and I stood gazing for some time lost in admiration of her beauty; quite forgetting the purpose for which I had come. I thought, she is, after all, the lady of my heart. If I do not obtain her, Kama (the Hindu god of love) will not suffer me to live; but how can I make known my love to her? Were I now to wake her, she would start up with a cry of alarm, and I should probably lose my life. I must think of some other way of letting her know my love.

Then, looking round, I saw laid on a shelf a thin board prepared for painting, and a box of paints and brushes. With these I made a hasty sketch of the princess as she lay, and of myself kneeling at her feet; and underneath it I wrote this verse,

> "Of thee, thy slave in humble attitude thus prays:
> Sleep on! not worn, like me, by pervading love."

I then painted on the wall near her a pair of chakravakas, or kind of turtle dove, in loving attitude, gently took off her ring, replacing it with mine, and slipped out without disturbing any of the sleepers.

There was at that time among the prisoners a man named Sinhagosha, formerly a chief officer of police, but now imprisoned through a false accusation made by Kanṭaka. With this man I had already made acquaintance, and I now went to him, and told him how I had killed Kantaka. With his consent, I went forth from the prison, and walked away with Sringalika. We had not gone far when we fell in with a patrol. I thought to myself I could easily run away from them, but what would become of the poor old woman, she would certainly be caught. Hastily determining, therefore, on what was best to be done, I walked right up to them with unsteady gait and idiotic look, and said, "Sirs, if I am a thief, kill me, but you have no right to touch this old woman."

She, perceiving my intention, came up, and very humbly said: "Honoured sirs, this young man is my son. He has been for some time confined as a lunatic, but was supposed to be cured, and I brought him home yesterday. In the middle of the night, however, he started up, and calling out, 'I will kill Kantaka, and make love to the king's daughter,' rushed out into the street. I have at last overtaken him, and am trying to take him home. Will you be so good as to help me, and tie his hands behind him, that he may not get away again."

As she said this, I called out, "Oh, old woman, who ever bound a god or the wind? Shall these crows catch an eagle?" and then started off at full speed. She, renewing her entreaties, begged them to pursue me, but they only laughed at her, and said, "Do you think we have nothing to do but to run after madmen. You must be as mad as he is to have taken him out," and so they went on their way.

I stopped when I found I was not pursued. She soon overtook me, and we went to my house, to the great joy of my wife, who had scarcely hoped for my deliverance.

In the morning I saw Dhanamittra, told him all that had happened, and thanked him for following my directions so implicitly.

After this I went to the forest to see Marichi. I found him restored to his former condition, and able to give me the desired information. From him I learnt that you would be here about this time.

In the morning after my escape, Sinhagosha informed the king of what happened, and how Kantaka had been killed when about to enter the princess's apartments. Being found to be innocent of the crime of which he was accused, he was appointed governor of the prison in Kantaka's place. Before the underground passage was filled up, he permitted me to pass through it more than once to see the princess, who was favourably disposed towards me through the picture and verse, and still more by all that Sringalika had said in my favour.

No great search was made after me, and by keeping quiet and going out only at night I escaped further arrest.

My lord, you know how Chandavarma besieged Champa, and how Sindavarma was defeated and taken prisoner. When I heard this, and how the conqueror intended to force the princess to marry him, I went to Dhanamittra and said, "Do you go about among the ministers and officers of the imprisoned king, and to the principal citizens, and tell them to be ready to attack the enemy as soon as they hear of the death of Chandavarma; I will engage to kill him to-morrow."

How Dhanamittra has performed his part you have just seen. As to myself, I put on a dress suitable for the occasion, and as many persons were going in and out of the palace I managed to slip in unobserved, and get very near the intending bridegroom. Suddenly, stretching out my arm as he was about to take the hand of the princess, I gave him a mortal wound with a sword. Then saying a few hasty words of encouragement to her, I defended myself against those who endeavoured to seize me, till I heard your welcome voice, deep as the sound of thunder, and had the happiness of embracing you.

The other stories are full of incident and anecdote, but the specimen given is sufficient to show the nature of the work, which ends abruptly, and was apparently left unfinished by the author. Had he continued it, the ten faithful friends would probably have recovered the kingdom of Magadha, and replaced on its throne their good father and patron, the king Rajahansa and his queen Vasumati.

CHAPTER V.

THE BAITAL PACHISI, OR TWENTY-FIVE STORIES OF A DEMON.

AMONG the many adventures, tales, stories, and narratives given in the Katha-sarit-sagara (Chapter III.), there are also the plan and details of a collection of stories extremely popular in India, existing both in Sanscrit, and in all the vernacular dialects that have any literature—Hindi, Bengali, Mahratti, Guzerathi, Tamul, Telegoo, and the rest. These are known as the Vetala Panchavinsati, commonly called the Baital Pachisi, or Twenty-five Tales of a Demon, related by a sprite or demon, or vampire, who haunts cemeteries and animates dead bodies, to Vickramaditya, king of Oojein, according to the usual version; to Trivikrama Sena, king of Prelishthana or Pythan, on the Godaveri, according to the Katha-sagara. Whether it was a separate work originally, or whether it always formed the ninth section of the twelfth book of the Katha is uncertain. Anyhow, it is now printed separately, and has been translated into English by Raja Kali Krushna, of Calcutta, Mr. Eastwick, Captain Hollings, Munshi Ghulam Mahomed, Captain Richard Burton, and Mr. John Platts. Of these translations Captain Burton's is the freest and the most amusing, and he says truly enough, "The merit of the old stories lies in their suggestiveness and their general applicability. I have ventured to remedy the conciseness of their language, and to clothe the skeleton with flesh and blood."

The tales were told under the following circumstances:—In the renowned city of Oojein there lived a king named Gandharb Sen, who had four sons. On his death he was succeeded by his eldest son, known as Shank. The said Shank was shortly afterwards slain by his younger brother, Vickram, who then became king, governed well, extended his dominions, and established an era. When he was well established on the throne, he thought to himself that he must travel a bit, and see the countries about which he was ever hearing. Accordingly, he handed over his government and his throne temporarily to his younger brother, Bhartari, and, assuming the guise of a devotee, set out on his wanderings.

Now, it happened that in that city there lived a pious Brahman, and a deity pleased with his austerities presented to him the fruit of immortality. Taking it home to his wife, he told her that whoever ate the fruit would become immortal. She, however, did not seem at all pleased with the idea of immortality, and said that on the whole it was better to die and escape from the trials of the world, than to go on living for ever and begging alms. The Brahman then asked her what he had better do with the fruit. She said, "Give it to the king, and ask for wealth in exchange, and then we shall enjoy the advantages of this world, as well as those of the world to come." Hearing this, the Brahman went to the king, and explained the circumstances of the case. The king gave him a lakh of rupees and dismissed him, and then went straight to the queen whom he loved most, and gave her the fruit and told her to eat it, and remain young and beautiful for ever. The queen thanked the king in the way that only woman can, and he departed. But it happened that, though the queen loved the king much, she loved a certain ambassador more; so, when opportunity offered, she presented the fruit to him in a manner at least as tender as that with which it had been offered to her. The ambassador took it, but, though he liked the queen, he really loved one of her maids of honour, so he gave the fruit to her. She, being an ambitious girl, thought that it was a fitting present for the king, and that to give it to him was the best thing that she could do with it. Accordingly she went and presented it to the king, who took it, and dismissed her with much wealth and with many thanks. Knowing then that his great love for the queen was not returned, and awakening from his dream of unbounded affection, he entered the female apartments, and asked the queen what she had done with the fruit he gave her. She replied at once, "I ate it up." The king then showed her the fruit, and she was speechless. He then left her, washed the fruit, and ate it himself, and, abandoning the kingdom and the throne, assumed the guise of a devotee, and telling no one, went forth alone to the jungle to meditate over the vanities of the humanities, of which the love of woman is one.

The throne of Vickram was vacant. When this news reached king Indra, he sent a demon to watch over the city by day and by night, and this he did faithfully. The news, however, spread from country to country that king Bhartari had abandoned his government and gone away as an ascetic. In time, king Vickram heard it too, and immediately set out to return to his country. He arrived at his capital at midnight, and as he entered the city he was challenged by the demon, who called out, "Who art thou, and whither goest thou? Stand and give your name." The king said, "It is I, king Vickram; I am entering my own city; who art thou to challenge me?" The demon replied, "The deities have sent me to guard this city; if you are really king Vickram, first fight me, and then enter the city." On this the king and the demon fought, and the former threw the latter, and sat upon his breast. The demon then said, "Oh! king, thou hast thrown me; I grant thy life as a boon." On this the king laughing, said, "Thou art mad; it is for me to grant life to you; how canst thou now grant it to me? The demon replied, "Oh! king, I am about to save thee from death; first listen to my tale, and then rule over the whole world free from care." The king agreed, and the demon spoke as follows:—

"In this city there once reigned a very liberal king, named Chandrabhau. One day in the jungle he beheld an ascetic hanging head downwards from a tree, and sustaining himself by inhaling smoke alone, neither receiving anything from any one, nor speaking a word to a soul. On his return home, the king said, 'Whoever will bring this ascetic to me here shall receive a lakh of rupees.' A courtesan, hearing these words, came to the king and said, 'If I obtain your majesty's leave, I will have a child by that ascetic, and bring it here mounted on his shoulder.' The king agreed to her proposal, and she started for the jungle, where she found the ascetic withered up, neither eating nor drinking, and hanging head downwards. The courtesan prepared some sweetmeats, and put it into his mouth, while he, finding it agreeable, ate it up eagerly. She applied a little more to his mouth, and for two days continued to feed him with the same, and by eating it he gained a little strength. Then opening his eyes, and descending from the tree, he asked her, 'On what business hast thou come hither?'

"The courtesan replied, 'I am the daughter of a god. I have been practising religious austerities in heaven, but have now come to this jungle to enjoy myself.' The ascetic said, 'Where is your hut? show it to me.' She then took him to her hut, and began to feed him with delicious food, and this he took daily. Soon the god of love troubled him, and forgetting his vows, he was imprudent, and lost the reward of penance. The woman conceived. In ten months a boy was born, and, when he was some months old, she said to the hermit, 'Oh, holy man, now let us go and perform pilgrimages, by which all the sins of the flesh may be blotted out.'

"Deluding him with such words, she placed the boy on his shoulder, and started for the king's court to show that she had earned her money. The king seeing her at a distance, and also the child on the shoulder of the devotee, said to his courtiers, 'See, this is the very same woman who went out to bring in the devotee.' They replied, 'O king, you are right; it is the woman, and she has fulfilled what she promised to do.'

"When the ascetic heard these remarks of the king and the courtiers, he thought that they had done this to destroy his penance. He therefore left the palace, went out of the city, and, having killed the boy, retired to another forest to perform his devotions. After some time that king died, and the devotee completed his penance.

"The short of the story is this, that you three men have been born under one asterism, one conjunction, and in one moment. You were born in a king's house; the second was an oilman's child; the third, the devotee, in the house of a potter. You govern here, while the oilman's son was the ruler of the infernal regions; but the potter's son, bringing his religious meditations to thorough perfection, has killed the oilman's child, and turned him into a demon in a burning ground, and placed him, hanging head downwards, on a siras tree, and he is now intent on killing you. If you escape, you will rule the world. I have informed you of all these things; do not be careless with respect to them."

The demon then departed, and the king entered his palace. The next day he held a general court, at which there was a large attendance of his subjects, and great joy was exhibited by everybody in the city at his return.

One day an ascetic, named Shantsil, appeared at the court with a fruit in his hand, and presented the same to the king. He then spread a cloth, sat down for a short time, and then went away. On his departure, the king thought that this might be the person of whom the demon spoke. With this suspicion in his mind, he did not eat the fruit, but gave it to his steward, and told him to keep it carefully. The devotee, however, came constantly in the same way, and left a fruit every time. Now, one day, it happened that the king went to his stables. The ascetic came there also, and presented the king with a fruit in the usual way. While tossing it in the air, it fell to the ground, and a monkey took it up and broke it into pieces. So exquisite a ruby came out of it, that the king and his attendants were astonished at its brilliance. The king then said to the devotee, "Why have you given me this ruby?" The latter replied, "It is not proper according to the written religious law to go empty-handed to certain places, or to certain persons. Each of the fruits that I presented to you contains a jewel." The steward was then ordered to bring them all, and each was found to contain a ruby of such excellence that their value was incredible.

The king then asked the religious mendicant for an explanation of the object of these gifts. The ascetic, after quoting certain things, of which it is improper to speak in public, said, "That he would tell him in private," and added, "It is a rule that whatever is heard by three pair of ears (*i.e.*, by three persons), remains no secret; the words which reach two pair of ears (*i.e.*, two persons), no man hears; while the contents of one pair of ears (*i.e.*, the knowledge of one person) are unknown to Brahma himself, not to speak of man."

The king then took him apart, and asked him what he really wanted. The ascetic said, "Sire, I am about to practise magical arts in a large body-burning ground on the banks of the river, by which I shall acquire supernatural powers. I beg of you to pass one whole night with me, and by your being near me, my magic arts will succeed." The king asked on what day he should come, and this being told him, he said, "You can go; I will assuredly come, and alone." When the time came, he went and found the ascetic sitting and beating two skulls together by way of music, and surrounded by goblins, evil spirits, and witches in various frightful shapes, all dancing around. The king felt no alarm, but simply asked, "What do you want me to do?" The devotee replied, "About four miles south of this place is a burning ground; there you will find a siras tree (*Mimosa serisa*), on which a corpse is suspended; bring that corpse to me here." Amidst many difficulties the king at last arrived at the spot, and found the corpse fastened by a string, and hanging head downwards. Having climbed up the tree and cut him down, he was surprised to hear him weep aloud, and again climb up the tree and suspend himself as before. The king went after him, and brought him down again, and clutching him under his arm, said, "Vile wretch, tell me who thou art?" The corpse made no reply, and then the king thought to himself, "This, perhaps, is the very oilman's son whom the demon said the devotee had deposited in the place where bodies are burnt." Thinking thus, he bound him up in his mantle, and started off to return to the devotee.

Then the sprite who was animating the corpse spoke out, and asked, "Who art thou, and whither art thou taking me?" The king replied, "I am king Vickram, and am taking thee off to a devotee." The sprite said, "I will go on one condition, if thou utterest a word on the way I will come straight back." The king agreed, and went off with him. On the way the sprite said, "O king, those who are learned, clever, and wise, their days are passed in the delight of song and the pleasure of reading; while the days of the unwise and the foolish are spent in dissipation and sleep. It is better that this long journey should be enlivened by profitable discourse. Listen to the story I am going to tell you."

The sprite then tells twenty-four stories, and at the end of each he asks the king a question concerning it, to which he invariably replies, and having thus broken the contract of silence, the sprite returns, and suspends himself on the same tree. The king again cuts him down, binds him up in a bundle, and placing him on his shoulder again starts off. This occurs twenty-four times, but on the conclusion of the twenty-fifth tale, the king through ignorance holds his tongue. The sprite then said with great glee, "Your majesty, I have been highly pleased at witnessing your patience and your courage," and then proceeded to warn him against Shantsil, the devotee who had sent the king on this errand, and was anxious to kill him on his return. "You will see," he said, "that he will ask you to prostrate yourself so that eight parts of your body will touch the ground. When he proposes this to you, say that you are the king of kings, and do not understand how to bow in adoration to any one. Ask him to show you how to do it, and when he bows down, sever his head from his body with your sword. If you do this you will reign uninterruptedly, but if he kills you he will reign permanently." Having thus warned the king, the sprite came out of the corpse, and went his way.

The king then returned with the body, and placed it before the ascetic, who being much pleased, praised the king. After making various sacrifices the devotee asked the king to make obeisance, but the king remembering the words of the sprite, and joining his hands together, said with great humility, "O priest, I know not how to perform obeisance; you, however, are a spiritual teacher, if you will show me how to do it, I shall perform it." The ascetic on hearing this lowered his head to prostrate himself, and the king seizing the opportunity severed his head from his body with one blow of the sword. It is declared that there is nothing unlawful in slaying him who would himself slay another.

After this, Indra and the rest of the gods, having witnessed the king's courage, mounted their cars and began to raise shouts of victory. Indra then said to the good king Vickram, "Ask a boon, and it will be granted." The king replied, "Your majesty, let this story concerning me become famous in the world." Indra answered, "So long as the moon, sun, earth, and sky endure, this story shall be famous, and thou shalt be the ruler over the whole earth."

The king then threw the two corpses into the oil cauldron, and thereupon they appeared as two heroes, and presented themselves saying, "What command is there for us?" The king replied, "When I remember you, then do you come." Having taken from them their promise to do this, the king returned home, and attended more than ever to his government.

Out of the twenty-five stories, three will serve as specimens of the whole.

I.—ABOUT A WOMAN'S PROMISE.

In the city of Madanpur there reigned a king, named Birbar. In the same city there lived a trader, called Hermyadutt, who had a daughter, by name Madansena. One day, in the season of spring, she went with her female friends to a garden, and when there met a young man, named Somdatt, the son of the merchant Dharmdatt. This young man fell violently in love with her at first sight, and involuntarily went up to her, and, taking hold of her hand, began to say, "If thou wilt not love me, I shall abandon my life on thy account." The girl said, "You must not do so, for in doing this you will commit a great sin." Somdatt replied, "Excessive love has pierced my heart. The fear of separation has burnt up my body. From the pain all my memory and intellect are lost, and at present, through my excess of love, I have no regard for virtue or sin. If you will give me a promise, I shall hope to live." Madansena said, "On the fifth day from this I am going to be married, then I shall first meet you, and after that I shall go with my husband." Having given this promise, and affirming it by oath, she went home.

On the fifth day after this she was married, and her husband took her to his house. After several days her sisters-in-law forcibly took her to her husband at night, but she would have nothing to do with him; and, when he wished to embrace her, she jerked him with her hand, and told the story of her promise to the merchant's son. Hearing this, her husband said, "If thou truly wishest to go with him, then go."

Having thus obtained her husband's consent, she put on her best clothes and jewels, and started for the merchant's house. On her way she met a thief, who asked her where she was going alone at that midnight hour so adorned. She replied, "That she was going to meet her lover." On hearing this, the thief said, "Who is your protector here?" She replied, "Kama, the god of love, with his weapons is my protector." She then told the whole story to the thief, and said, "Do not spoil my attire. I promise you that, on my return, I will give you up all my jewels."

The thief let her go, and she proceeded to the place where Somdatt was lying asleep. Awaking him suddenly, he arose bewildered, and asked her who she was, and why she had come. She replied, "I am the daughter of the merchant Hermyadutt. Do you not remember that you forcibly took my hand in the garden, and insisted on my giving you my oath, and I swore, at your bidding, that I would leave the man I was married to, and come to you. I have come accordingly; do to me whatever thou pleasest."

Somdatt asked her if she had told the story to her husband, and she said that she had told him all, and that he had allowed her to come. The youth said: "This affair is like jewels without apparel; or food without clarified butter; or singing out of tune; all these things are alike. In the same way, dirty garments take away beauty, bad food saps the strength, a wicked wife takes away life, a bad son ruins the family. What a woman does not do is of little moment, for she does not give utterance to the thoughts of her mind; and what is at the tip of her tongue she does not reveal, and what she does, she does not tell of. God has created a woman in the world as a wonder."

After uttering these words, the merchant's son said: "I will have nothing to do with the wife of a stranger." Hearing this, she returned homeward. On her way she met the thief, and told him the whole story. He applauded her highly, and let her go, and she went to her husband and related to him the whole circumstance. Her husband, however, evinced no affection for her, but said, "The beauty of the cuckoo consists in its note alone; the beauty of a woman consists in her fidelity to her husband; the beauty of an ugly man is his knowledge; the beauty of a devotee is his patient suffering."

Having related so much, the sprite said, "O king! whose is the highest merit of these three?" Vickram replied: "The thief's merit is the greatest." "How," asked the sprite? The king answered: "Seeing that her heart was set on another man, the husband let her go; through fear of the king, Somdatt let her alone; whereas there was no reason for the thief leaving her unmolested; therefore the thief is superior." Hearing this, the sprite returned again and suspended himself on that tree. The king also went there, again took him down, and having bound him, placed him on his shoulder, and once more carried him away.

II.—OF THE FATAL EFFECTS OF LOVE.

There is a city named Bishalpur, the king of which was called Bipuleshwar. In this city there lived a merchant whose name was Arthdatt, and he had a daughter, Anangmanjari. She was married to a merchant of Kauwalpur, by name Munici. Some time after the marriage the merchant went a trading to a distant land, and the wife remained at home. One day when she was standing in her summer-house, and looking on the road, there passed by a young Brahman named Kamlekar. The eyes of the two met, and they became enamoured of each other at first sight.

After recovering his self-possession, on account of the restlessness caused by the separation from his beloved, the Brahman went to the house of his friend. The woman, too, was exceedingly uneasy, and was found by a female companion in a state of insensibility. The companion sprinkled rose water over her, and caused her to smell perfumes. When she came round, and her senses returned, she said, "Oh, Kama,* Maradev burnt thee to ashes, and yet thou wilt not desist from thy knavish tricks, but comest and inflictest pain on innocent, feeble women!"

Uttering these words, evening came on, and the

---

* Kama, in Hindu mythology, is the god of love, and answers to our Cupid. He is represented as a beautiful youth, the most lovely of all the gods, holding a bow and flower-tipped arrows, with which, while wandering through perfumed glades, accompanied by Rati, his spouse, he wounds the hearts of the inhabitants of the three worlds. He has various names, such as Ananga, the Incorporeal; Smara, the Ideal, as the son of Maya or Illusion. Sir William Jones says of him, "He appears evidently the same as the Grecian Eros and the Roman Cupido; but the Indian description of his person and arms, his family attendants, and attributes, has new and peculiar beauties."

moon appeared. While gazing at the moonlight, she said, "O moon, I used to be told that the water of life is in you, and that you shed it in your beams; to-day, however, even you have begun to pour down venom." She then said to her companion, "Take me up, and lead me away from this place, for I am being burnt to death by the moonlight." The companion took her away, saying at the same time, "Dost thou feel no shame at uttering such words?" Then she said, "O friend, I am fully aware of all, but Kama has wounded me and rendered me void of shame. I make great efforts to be patient; but the more I continue to be consumed with the fire of separation, the more venom-like does home appear to me." The companion said, "Keep thy mind at ease, I will relieve thee of all thy suffering."

Having said this, the companion went home, and the love-sick one determined in her mind that she would quit this body for the sake of her beloved, and being born again enjoy life with him. With this longing in her mind, she threw a noose around her neck, and was about drawing it tight, when the companion returned. The latter, instantly taking the rope off her neck, said, "Everything can be attained by living, and nothing by dying." The love-sick one replied, "It is better to die than to suffer such pain." The companion said, "Repose awhile, I will go and bring him."

Having said this, she went to the place where Kamlekar was, and looking at him, perceived that he also was much disturbed by the separation from his beloved. His friend was mixing sandal in rose-water and applying it to his body, and fanning him with the tender leaves of the plantain tree. Despite which, all aflame with passion, he was crying out and saying to his friend, "Bring me poison, I will sacrifice my life, and be released from this suffering." Observing his state, she said to herself, "However courageous, learned, sagacious, discreet, and patient a man may be, Kama reduces him to a state of distraction all the same." These thoughts having passed through her mind, the companion said to him, "O Kamlekar, Anangmanjari has sent word to thee to come and bestow life on her." He replied, "She, indeed, has given life to me."

After saying this he rose up, and the companion took him along with her to the love-sick lady. When he got there, lo! she was lying dead. Thereupon he uttered a cry of anguish, and his spirit also fled. When morning came, her household took both of them to the burning ground, and arranging the pile, placed them on it together, and set fire to it. In the meantime her husband, who had just returned from abroad, also came to the burning ground. Hearing the sound of the people's weeping, he went there, and what does he see but his wife burning with a strange man. He also, being distracted with love, burnt himself to death in the same fire. The people of the city hearing the news, began saying, one to the other, "Neither has eye seen, nor ear heard of so wonderful an event."

After relating so much of the story, the sprite said, "O king, of these three whose love was the greatest?" The king said, "Her husband was the deepest lover." "Why?" asked the sprite. The king replied, "He, who seeing his wife dead for another's sake, put aside anger, and cheerfully laid down his life through love for her; he is the deepest lover." Hearing these words, the sprite went back and hung himself again on that tree. The king too went there, and having bound him, placed him once more on his shoulder, and carried him off.

III.—OF A QUEER RELATIONSHIP.

There is a city in the south named Dhurumpoor, the king of which was named Mahabal. Once upon a time another king of the same region led an army against him, and invested his capital. After much fighting Mahabal was defeated, and, taking his wife and daughter with him, he fled by night into the jungle. After travelling several miles the day broke, and a village came in view. Leaving the queen and princess seated beneath a tree, he himself went to the village to get something to eat, and in the meantime a band of Bhils, or hill robbers, came and surrounded him, and told him to throw down his arms.

The king, on hearing this, commenced discharging arrows at them, and the Bhils did the same from their side. After fighting for some time, an arrow struck the king's forehead with such force that he reeled and fell, and one of the Bhils came up and cut off his head. When the queen and the princess saw that the king was dead, they went back into the jungle weeping and beating their breasts. After going some distance they became tired and sat down, and began to be troubled with anxiety.

Now, it happened that a king named Chandrasen, together with his son, while pursuing game, came into that very jungle, and the king, noticing the footprints of the two women, said to his son, "How have the footprints of human feet come into this vast forest?" The prince replied, "These are women's footprints, a man's foot is not so small." The king said, "Come let us look for them, and if we find them I will give her whose foot is the largest to thee, and I will take the other for myself." Having entered into this mutual compact, they went forward, and soon perceived the two women seated on the ground. They were delighted at finding them, and seating them on their horses in the manner agreed upon, they brought them home. The prince took possession of the queen, as her feet were the largest, and the king took the princess, and they were married accordingly.

Having related so much the sprite said, "Your majesty, what relationship will there be between the children of these two?" On hearing this, the king held his tongue through ignorance, being unable to describe the relationship. On which, the contract of silence having been observed, the sprite came out of the corpse, and went his way, as described previously.

CHAPTER VI.

THE SINHASANA DWATRINSATIKA, OR THE THIRTY-TWO STORIES OF THE SPEAKING STATUES.

THE Sinhasana Dwatrinsatika is a collection of thirty-two stories (author and date unknown), which were related by thirty-two statues forming the pedestal of a throne belonging to the renowned Vickramaditya, king of Oojein, and told under the following circumstances:—

In the city of Oojein there lived a king named Bhoj, who was powerful, rich, illustrious, and virtuous. A description of his many good qualities are then given, followed by a description of his city and its inhabitants, its bazaars, houses, public buildings, and markets.

In a garden near the city there dwelt a market gardener, who erected a platform in the middle of his property, for the purpose of sitting there, and protecting his produce from thieves and birds. Whenever the man ascended this platform he was seized, like many other people who ascend platforms, with a sort of madness, and used to abuse in most violent language the good king Bhoj. Although frequently beaten by the by-standers and passers-by, it had no effect, and he still continued, when on the platform, to give utterance to foolish talk, and to inveigh against the king. This circumstance was at last reported to the Rajah, who determined to go to the spot; and having gone there, concealed himself, and quietly sat down. As soon as the gardener mounted the platform, he began to say: "Let my people proceed forthwith, seize Rajah Bhoj in his fort, put him to death, and recover my kingdom from him quickly, by doing which they will obtain both fame and future reward."

On hearing this the king was struck with terror, and returned home. On the following day he sent for the learned men and the astrologers, and related to them the story of the preceding night. The astrologers having consulted together, and calculated the day, hour, and minute said: "Rajah! in our calculation there is some indication of wealth." The learned men said: "In this place there is an immense treasure."

The king then ordered the place to be dug up and thoroughly examined. On the earth being removed four feet of a throne became visible, but it was found impossible to move the same. A Pundit, or learned man, suggested that a sacrifice should be offered, and that then the throne would be easier to move. This being done, the local deity accepted the sacrifice, and no sooner was hand then laid upon it than the throne was raised. Having been dusted and cleaned, it was set up, and the king was delighted with it. When the throne was freed from earth, dirt, and dust, washed and wiped, it began to shine so that no one's eyes could rest upon it. Whoever saw that throne studded with jewels, beheld the spectacle of God's glory.

It had been so constructed that the like of it had never been seen or heard of before. Eight statues were carved on each of its four sides, each of them holding a lotus flower in its hand. If angels or saints had seen it, they also would have been struck with amazement.

The king then ordered the throne to be thoroughly

repaired, and in the course of five months it was completely finished. The statues were so well repaired and set up that they looked as if they were about to speak or to walk. From head to foot they were full of beauty, their eyes were like the gazelle's, their waists were as slender as the leopard's, the motion of their feet was like the gait of the swan. Whosoever beheld their countenances imprinted them on the pupils of their eyes.

Having seen the throne, the Pundits, or learned men, began to give the king a true account of it. "O Rajah," they said, "life and death are in the power of God, but it is desirable for a man to enjoy all the pleasures of existence during his lifetime." Hearing this the king was much pleased, and began to say, "Perhaps God has made these statues with his own hand, or the dancing-girls are from the court of Indra." He then ordered the learned men to calculate the auspicious hour and lucky moment for him to ascend the throne.

The day having been fixed, the gods having been propitiated, the people having been feasted, and gifts having been bestowed upon all, the king approached the throne, and advancing his right foot, was about to place it thereon, when all the statues burst out into an uncontrollable fit of laughter. The Rajah became confused, and starting back was much abashed and somewhat frightened, and perplexed to know how these lifeless images became animated. With indignation and fury he withdrew his foot, and asked the statues to explain why they laughed.

The first among the statues, whose name was Rattanmunjari, then spoke, and began to relate the tale of the great and mighty Vickram who had obtained the throne. The story is somewhat to the same effect as that told about him in the previous chapter of the Baital Pachisi, interspersed with reflections such as these: "Rajah Bhoj, listen to these words. If God be inclined to mercy, then will he change a straw into a mountain, and if to wrath, then will he reduce the mountain to a straw. Whatsoever is written in the book of destiny, the same never turns out false. At the moment of conception in his mother's womb, a man brings with him four things—viz., gain, loss, pain, and pleasure. He may wander through the three worlds, *i.e.*, earth, water, and air, or the fourteen abodes of Brahma and of the other deities, but whatever is written in fate nothing shall efface it." The statue then relates how this throne was given to Vickram by the Rajah Bahu Bul, and how he reigned prosperously, and established an era.

Every day the Rajah approached the throne, and advanced his foot to ascend it, and each day one of the statues addressed him, and told him that he was not worthy to sit upon it, and that only a person resembling Vickram in every way could aspire to such a place.

Each statue then tells a story describing the bravery, the devotion, the generosity, the noble-heartedness, the greatness, and the many virtues of the mighty Vickram, and by the time each story is finished, the propitious hour for the Rajah to ascend the throne has passed away. This is repeated daily until each of the thirty-two statues has told her tale, many of them very monotonous, and, as in the case of biographies of all great men, one would like to hear something of the vices as well as of the virtues of the hero. Finally, the Rajah Bhoj orders the throne to be buried again in the place where it was found, and entrusting all state affairs to his chief minister, and abdicating his throne, he goes on pilgrimages, becomes a devotee, and leads the life of an ascetic.

Of the stories told by the statues, a few have been selected as specimens of the whole lot.

I.—OF VICKRAM'S VISIT TO THE INFERNAL REGIONS, AND THE FOUR GEMS; RELATED BY THE SEVENTEENTH STATUE, SATYAVATI.

Listen, Rajah Bhoj. One day Vickram seated himself upon his throne, like Indra in his court. The musicians played on their instruments, the dancing-girls went through their songs and movements, the bards shouted the praises of the king, while the Brahmans recited the hymns of the Vedas. Wrestlers were ready to engage in athletic contests, while the menagerie of animals was full of beasts. In short, there was to be found everything worthy of a princely court. The king was surrounded by many learned and intelligent persons, and his reception room was furnished with every necessary. Vickram then spoke to the Pundits as follows:—"Hear what I say, 'Indra is the king of heaven, and is well acquainted with everything connected with us mortals, but who is the king of the lower regions, and where does he live?'" A Brahman replied, "O, Maharajah, or great king, Sheshanaga is the king of the regions below the earth, and he has one hundred necks. His queen is called Pudamini, and he is altogether free from disease and sorrow. Joy reigns supreme in his dominions, and happiness is everlasting there."

Vickram then signified his wish to pay him a visit, and summoning the demons he was at once transported to the palace of the king of Patala, or the lower regions. The place is then described as a mansion made of gold and studded with precious stones, which sent forth such a dazzling light that it was difficult to distinguish between day and night.

Wreaths of lotus flowers were suspended across the gateway, and general rejoicing was observed everywhere. The interview with the king Sheshanaga is then told, and Vickram is hospitably entertained for several days. On his departure the king of the lower regions presents him with four gems, and relates their respective qualities. One of these jewels, he said, will produce at a moment's notice as many ornaments as you may require; the other will produce elephants, horses, palanquins, honours, titles, and fame; from the third you can get any amount of wealth; and the fourth will assist you in offering prayers and in practising virtue. On his way home Vickram met a poor Brahman, who said, "I am hungry, give me some alms that I may support my family." The king replied, "I have got four jewels with me, and each has such and such particular qualities. You can have whichever you like. The Brahman asked permission to go home first, and consult his family before giving a final reply. On arriving at his place he told his wife, his son, and his daughter-in-law about the offer made to him, and the peculiarities of the gems. The wife at once said: "Fetch the jewel that brings money, and do away with every other thought, for wealth brings friends, ample means, religious merit, learning, piety and charity; you should not have a wavering mind, go and get that gem." The son then spoke and said: "What is the use of riches if they are not accompanied with greatness and its necessary provisions. When a man is possessed of all these, then he is respected by everybody, his enemies even look on him with awe, and he makes a name in the world. Try to procure that precious stone which carries with it dignity and fame, for it is useless to live on the surface of the earth without being distinguished."

In the meantime the daughter-in-law said to him, "Bring me the jewel which produces ornaments, for they beautify a woman and adorn a maid to such an extent that they look like fairies, and then in adverse circumstances they can be sold and will produce much money. Oh, father-in-law, do not waste time. You are endowed with common sense, while my husband is crazy, and my mother-in-law is senseless. I beg of you to bring that gem, which will supply us with all kinds of jewels." On hearing their speeches the Brahman replied, "All of you seem to be mad. I want nothing but religion, which gives a man real power, fulfils his desires, and makes him distinguished. The soul of a religious person becomes immortal, and self-conceit departs from him. Happen what may, I shall stick to my religion, which shall not be shaken in any way by you."

The four persons thus expressed their peculiar ideas, and, as they could not agree, the Brahman returned to the king and said, "O Maharaj, I went home to consult the people of my house, but nothing has come of it. We are at variance with each other, and each has his own standard of judging things, and we could not come to any unanimous conclusion." The king replied: "Do not be disappointed, I will give you all the four gems, which you can take home, and it will be a happy thing for me, that you and all the members of your family should remain satisfied with my gift." In short, the king generously presented the four jewels to the Brahman, who blessed him and returned home. Oh, Rajah Bhoj, in such a lordly manner did Vickram give alms, and in the point of charity who can be compared to him in this iron age?

II.—THE STORY RELATED BY AMIPAREKHA, THE TWENTY-SECOND STATUE, CONCERNING THE STATE OF THE MIND OF FOUR BOYS BROUGHT UP ALONE.

O Rajah, put your anxieties aside, and listen to a narrative which I am about to relate. One day Vickramajita was in his Durbar, or audience hall, and asked his minister whether the understanding of man was predetermined by fate, or taught by his parents. The minister replied that the intellect was predestined by the Creator in accordance with what had happened in a previous existence, and that the father and mother had nothing to do with the capacity of the reasoning faculty. "O Maharaja, a man cannot be learned unless he has an inclination that way, or is destined to be so. No one can avoid his fate, even if he adopted innumerable measures to alter it." "O minister," replied the king, "what do you say? It is palpable in this world that from the time a child is born he imitates his parents in everything that he sees them do, or hears them say. What, then, has destiny to do with it? The child learns what he is taught, and his understanding follows the company that he keeps." On this the minister answered, "O incarnation of justice, I cannot be compared to you; but one should always bear in mind that a person obtains everything, whether good or bad, by fulfilling his destiny according to his lot." The king desired him to verify the statement, and with this view he ordered a palace to be built in such a dense forest that no human voice was ever heard there. As soon as a prince was born, the king sent him there in charge of a nurse who was deaf and dumb. In the same way the youthful son of the minister, of the magistrate, and of a Brahman were sent to the same place. The building was then surrounded at a distance of four miles by such a strong guard that nobody could pass that way, and was so isolated that no noise could reach it. At the end of twelve years the wife of the Brahman said to her husband, "I have lived now for a long time without my son, and, in case I die before I see him, my desire would not be fulfilled. Go to the king, and tell him that you have not seen the face of your son for twelve years, and that now you wish to become an ascetic, and spend the remaining portion of your days in religious observances, and would fain leave the management of the house to the boy before starting to the necessary shrines." The Brahman acted accordingly, and the king directed the minister to bring the boys to him. The minister himself went to the place and brought the prince first, whose nails were untrimmed, hair shaggy, and body dirty. The king looked at him and said, "O son, are you well and happy? where have you been so long, and whence have you come here? Give me an account of your life." The prince smiled and said, "It is due to your merits that I am happy in every way, and this is an auspicious day with me, as I have paid my respects to you." The son of the minister having been asked the same questions by the king, replied, "O Maharaja, where is anything like happiness to be found? One is born in this world, and after a longer or shorter career departs. As a vessel, placed in the water, gradually fills and sinks to the bottom, in the same way man lives and dies. He thinks that he whiles away his days, but the days know that they beguile him, and while he is temporary, they are eternal. Such is the way of the world, and how can I call myself happy?" In the same way the son of the magistrate, on being questioned, said, "O great king, we are on our guard both by day and by night, and still people commit thefts in the city, and our fame is tarnished without any fault on our part; how then can we say that we are happy?" The son of the Brahman was then sent for, and being asked a question regarding his health and happiness, replied, "I am sound in body, but how can I be happy? My life is being shortened day by day. One who lives to a good old age is said to be happy, but how can one be pleased when birth and death go hand in hand?" After hearing the words of these four youths, the king said to his minister, "The boys have answered according to their own ideas. It must be a fact that one cannot be made a learned man; but it is destiny or fate that makes a person follow any particular profession, and become illustrious or otherwise."

III.—THE STORY RELATED BY VIDYAVATI, THE TWENTY-SIXTH STATUE, ABOUT VICKRAM'S PENANCE AND SHIVA'S PROMISE.

O King! listen to the instructive story which I am about to relate. When man is born he does not bring anything with him into the world, neither does he carry anything away with him when he dies. The object of existence is that man should do something worthy of notice, and he will be duly compensated for his actions, whether good or bad. As life is transitory, a person should make a good figure in this world, so that he may enjoy a good name here and eternal felicity hereafter. Charity, sacred vows, and religious austerity practised in a former existence bear their fruit in a future one. Do not think of the money spent in a good cause, for this world of woes is an ocean, which can be safely crossed by no other means but charity, beneficence, and devotion. I have said that nothing would accompany man at the last. What did Raja

Harishchandra, King Kuriana, and Vickramajita take with them? The fame of the generous, the beneficent, and the pious is left to posterity, and they go to heaven after death. One day Vickram was in his court, and a female servant suggested that he should leave, as the time for worship was passing away. On hearing this, the king said to himself, "What she says is quite right; my life is daily being shortened, and I am wanting in knowledge, in virtues, and in devotion. It is better to abdicate the throne and practise meditation, so that I may do well in the next birth. I have wasted my energy in living as I have done, and in sustaining the life which resembles the dew that falls in the morning. My kingdom, my riches, and my attendants present only an illusion." With such thoughts in his mind he proceeded to a large forest, where he found some religious mendicants engaged in contemplation. They had lighted fires before them, and were burning themselves by slow degrees, and eventually consigned their whole bodies to the flames as an act of devotion. The king followed their example, and finally threw himself into the fire. Now, there was a temple close by dedicated to the god Shiva, whose attendant came out, and, having collected the ashes of the ascetics, placed them in different heaps; and then, in accordance with the orders of the god, he sprinkled the nectar of life upon the piles, so that the mendicants got up one by one and uttered the words, "Rama, Rama!" They then brought to notice that there had been another ascetic performing penance, but that he had not been animated. The Mahadev ordered this to be done, and Vickram was also restored to life. The ascetics were then dismissed with presents, and the god desired the king to ask for any blessing. Vickram replied, "Your goodness has supplied me with everything;

but I beg that you will liberate me from the transmigrations of the soul. As other devotees have been so freed by you, in the same way you can grant salvation to a wicked and wretched person like myself." The god Shiva praised Vickram's virtues, and told him to continue governing the mortals, and that he would free him at the time of his death. The king not assenting to this proposal, the god at last gave him a lotus flower, and said, "When this flower withers, then you will know that you must die in six months, and prepare accordingly." The king then returned to his city and his government, but did not tell the secret. After some years the lotus faded, and, with faith accepting the sign, he gave away his wealth to the Brahmans in charity, having first deducted the necessary properties for the maintenance of his wives and children, and for distribution among the beggars. This done, at the appointed time he died, and went straight to heaven.

CHAPTER VII.

VICKRAM-CHARITRA, OR THE ADVENTURES OF VICKRAMADITYA, KING OF OOJEIN.

IN Hindoo history there are so many Vickrams that it is impossible, in the total absence of dates, to distinguish one from the other. Whenever any author wanted to write a tale, a Vickram was generally taken as the hero, and his thoughts, words, and actions were served up in various ways. In our own early literature King Arthur and King Alfred were treated in much the same manner, and around them an halo of immortal glory has ever shone. Further adventures of this celebrated Vickram are given in a Prakrit poem by one Hurridas, the date of which is unknown. The work is interesting enough, and fully equal to many European fairy tales, and to the old stories of early heroes. It gives strong evidence of the belief of the Hindoos generally in the magic and occult powers of those who devote their lives to religious austerities and observances, and who, according to the popular idea, are able to accomplish anything, no matter how difficult or how improbable.

The story opens with a description of the king himself, of his city, of the happiness of his subjects, of his military talents, his intellectual accomplishments, and his love of justice. It goes on to relate the precautions taken to avert the effects of an adverse prediction made at his birth, that the

I 2

king would receive his death-blow from the hands of a person born of a virgin only seven years old.

The arrival of the hermit Sooden at the king's court is then announced, and from this great sage the king is anxious to obtain the knowledge of the art of transmigration, or the power of changing ourselves or others into any shape or form by the use of charms or spells. The hermit promises to teach him, and tells him to come alone to his dwelling after nightfall, and there learn the art. The king goes there alone for several nights consecutively, and is always followed unawares by a sentinel named Koobjuck, who conceals himself in the temple, and overhearing what passed between the king and the hermit, also became thoroughly acquainted with the mysteries of transmigration.

After this, the king determined to start on a journey to make inquiries himself about this wonderful virgin, whose son was to bring about his death. Leaving the kingdom in charge of the minister, he started on his travels, taking Koobjuck, the sentinel, with him. After travelling for some time, they arrived at a beautiful lake, where the camp was pitched, and the king, finding a dead serpent lying among the bushes, determined to test the efficacy of the hermit's instructions by causing his own soul to animate the body of the snake. Taking it to his tent, and telling Koobjuck, the sentinel, not to disturb him while he slept, he went through the usual formula, and soon the serpent began gradually to move, and started off into the adjoining woods. Koobjuck, the sentinel, had been watching the king, and determined also to test his knowledge on the subject. Accordingly, he assumed the form of the king, whose body was lying near him asleep, and came out of the tent before his retainers. He then mounted his horse, and returned with his followers to Oojein, personated the king, and assumed the reins of government; but, departing from his master's policy, he became as much hated as Vickram had formerly been loved.

In the meanwhile, the serpent king, after delicious wanderings in the woods, returned to the camp, and there, to his horror, discovered the body of Koobjuck alone in the place where he had left him, the king's body having departed. With much grief and lamentation, he abused the duplicity of his servant, and declining to appear in his form so full of deceit, ingratitude, and wickedness, he remained in the form of the serpent, and started for the city of Sendoornuggry. Journeying along, he came across the dead body of a parrot, and considering that it was both better and safer to be a parrot than a snake, he transformed himself into the parrot, and proceeded quickly to the town above mentioned. Outside the town he alighted on a tree under which were encamped a troop of Bahooroopees, a wandering tribe, who go about as dancers, actors, maskers, &c. They were in great distress at the failure of their performances, and were lamenting their hard fate and approaching ruin. The parrot spoke to them, and they became acquainted, and in the end he taught them how to effect the strangest metamorphosises, which produced the most extraordinary results, and gained them wonderful wealth. After this, the parrot desired the chief Bahooroopee to take him to the market, and sell him for his weight in gold. This the Bahooroopee objects to do, as it would show the greatest ingratitude on his part, and to illustrate this, tells the tale of the Alligator and the Traveller. After some further conversation between the two the matter is settled, and the parrot is sold to a wealthy merchant of the city, named Dushwant.

The domestic details of the merchant's household are then given, and the good effects produced by the residence of the parrot there. Subsequently a dancing-girl named Kamsaima endeavoured to extort money from the merchant by a false accusation. The attempt was frustrated by the ingenuity of the parrot, at which the girl was mortally offended, and after a time by her cunning and by getting into the merchant's bed-room at night, when his wife was sick, she finally prevailed upon him to make her a present of the bird. The merchant did this with the very greatest reluctance, but the parrot insisted on his doing it, adding that it was better, that he, the parrot, should run the risk of losing his life rather than that the merchant should violate his oath.

Once in the possession of the actress, she, to gratify her revenge, ordered her cook to kill the parrot and cook him, so that she might have the pleasure of eating him. The cook began to pluck the bird alive, and then leaving him for a moment to fetch a knife to cut his throat, the parrot king remembered Veytal the demon, and called on him to save his life. Veytal appears, and enables him to escape, and he takes refuge in a temple dedicated to the goddess Kalika, a renowned and sacred place not far distant from the city. When the cook returned and found the parrot gone, she got hold of another small bird which she cooked and served up to her mistress, who ate it all up with the happy thought that she was munching up her enemy.

After a few days the dancing-girl went to the temple to perform her devotions, and was addressed by the parrot in the character of the goddess Kalika, who promised to gratify her with anything that she might desire. To obtain this, however, she has to perform certain things before she can enter the paradise of Indra, where she was anxious to play and sing. The woman swallows everything, does what she is told to do, and finally finds that she has been sold, ridiculed and disgraced, and returned in the evening, naked, shaved, and her body covered with ashes, to her empty house; for, under the instructions of the goddess, she had given away the whole of her property to beggars and to Brahmans that morning.

The tale now reverts to Koobjuck, the sentinel whose soul animated king Vickram's body, and who was playing the devil with his subjects. A Brahman named Somedut, who came to his court, was badly treated by him, and having threatened him with the vengeance of heaven, set out in search of the real king Vickram. Journeying onward he arrived at a temple dedicated to Shiva, and there he met a young prince named Duntsain, who related to him his sorrows and his grief. It appeared that he was dying for love of the fair princess Pudmavuntty, to win whom it was necessary to bathe in a vessel filled with burning oil. Duntsain had attempted several times to go through the ordeal, but had not sufficient courage to proceed with it, and he said, "At the same time I love this princess too much to hope for any peace of mind while we remain apart from each other. I came down here to make another essay of my courage. My passion for her is daily gaining strength, and I cannot restrain it. Death would indeed be preferable to remaining in this dreadful state of agitation and suspense."

The Brahman, Somedut, promised to think over the case, and to assist him, and then proceeded in search of Vickram towards the city of Sendoornuggry, halting *en route* at the temple of the goddess Kalika. The parrot king, still living there, overheard the Brahman's lamentations and prayers concerning his lost sovereign. He began to converse with him, and, finally discovering himself, they set out together for Oojein. On their way they met the prince Duntsain at the temple of Shiva, and determined to engage in an attempt to gain for him the princess Pudmavuntty as his wife. To do this Vickram had to teach them the art of transmigration, and he turned himself into the Brahman, while the Brahman took the form of the parrot, and the three then proceeded to the dwelling of the princess. Vickram, in the guise of the Brahman, went forward, the prince and the parrot having been left outside, and announced that he had come to go through the ordeal required to gain the hand of the princess. This he does without sustaining any injury; and thus having won the princess, and become her master, he pleads the cause of the love-sick prince Duntsain. The princess agrees to accept him provided the Brahman succeeded in making her laugh and speak four times successively. The Brahman agreed to these terms, and summoned the Veytal or demon to assist him, and he promised to do what was needful.

The king Vickram, in the guise of the Brahman, now reposed within the splendid and sumptuous palace of the princess Pudmavuntty, and they were seated together. The spirit of the Veytal then transformed himself first into the form of a parrot that was painted on one of the panels of the wall, came down from the wall alive as a parrot, and related the history of king Bhudrasain, his son Soorsain, and the princess his wife. After this the Veytal assumed the form of a bird called the Shaloouky, or *Gracula religiosa*, and told them the story of the queen Shoodhamutty, her son Somunt, and the princess Mulattee. At the end of this tale he disappeared and returned in the shape of a peacock, and amused them with the history of king Rutnamanee, his son Sewdas, Hurridas the prime minister's son, and the princess Moheeny; and that being done he again departed, and finally re-appeared in the form of a peculiar description of swan, and commenced to relate the story of the princess Chitrangee and Charoo, the merchant's son. At the end of this tale he disappeared altogether, and the princess, having, during the recital of these stories, laughed and spoken four times, agreed to marry the prince Duntsain, who was then introduced. The celebration of the nuptials took place as soon as the necessary arrangements could be made to celebrate them with becoming splendour.

Vickram then departed from the palace along with the Brahman, Somedut, who was still in the form of the parrot, but shortly afterwards Vickram re-assumed the form of the parrot, and Somedut became himself again. The parrot then told Somedut to sell him to the king of Wishnoopoory, which he does for one hundred and twenty-five thousand rupees, and Somedut then returned to Oojein to tell the minister there that he had found Vickram, and to concert measures for his restoration to his throne.

Gopichund, the king of Wishnoopoory, was delighted with the parrot, and kept him in a magnificent cage, and took great pleasure in listening to the amusing tales which from time to time he recounted for the monarch's amusement. Eventually the parrot decided a most important case between a Zotinge, or goblin, and a Brahman's son, and received much praise for the same, while it introduced peace and happiness into the latter's family.

After this Somedut and Vickram's prime minister Bhutty, disguised as pious mendicants, arrived at Wishnoopoory, and attended a great sacrifice, which was brought about and ordered to be held under the following circumstances:—

The wise parrot and the good king Gopichund were one day engaged in conversing together, and they talked of the several sciences, the great benefits accruing from good government, and the necessity for leading a life of morality and virtue. After touching on these topics the parrot said, "My lord, I am extremely pleased to observe that, in the midst of the wealth and splendour with which you are surrounded, you are not indifferent to your future welfare. It behoves us all to have some thought of futurity. Your majesty spoke of a future state, surely enough we must prepare for it. This world is but transitory, and must sooner or later come to an end. With many it has already ended, and those who remain will soon run out their allotted period of existence. Thousands there are—in fact, they constitute by far the majority—who are content with the present, and who never look beyond this world. Alas! what can wealth or power, rank or position, avail a man at the last extremity? Only consider the object for which you have been created. Consider, again, in what will men who live solely for this world place their trust at their last end? Not in the bubble of worldly vanity—it will explode; not in worldly pleasures—they will vanish; not in high connections—they will not serve them; not in wealth—for they cannot carry it with them; not in rank or royal dignity—for death levels every distinction."

After more conversation in this style the parrot's serious talk on matters of religion made such an impression on the mind of the king that he begged the parrot to point out the most approved method of devotional exercise, so that he might, by following it, secure eternal happiness. The parrot replied: "There is a certain 'Rajasu yudna,' or sacrifice, which is performed only by great monarchs, attended by their tributary princes, and which should be performed in a certain manner. This would tend to confirm your majesty's faith and dependence on the great and supreme Ruler of the Universe." On this the astrologer and chief priest were sent for, and consulted on the subject; the former fixed upon an auspicious date for the commencement of the sacrifice, and the latter made the necessary arrangements.

After the sacrifice Somedut and Bhatty, still disguised, ask for the parrot, and the king gives him to them with very great reluctance, not liking to refuse the request of two such pious men, who had taken an important part in the recent ceremonies. They, taking the bird, hurry back to Oojein, and deliver him over to his wife, the queen, who conceals him in her apartments. The usurper Koobjuck, wishing to initiate the queen into the mysteries of transmigration, and thus gain her love and affection which had been hitherto refused, enters into the dead body of a hare, on which Vickram instantly resumes his own body, causes the hare to be destroyed, and re-ascends the throne.

The inhabitants of Oojein once more enjoyed the blessing of good government under king Vickram, and happiness reigned supreme. The king's mind, however, was constantly disturbed by reflecting on the prediction that he would be killed by the son of a very youthful virgin, and he sent emissaries into various countries to make inquiries about such persons.

The story is then told about Soometra, the youthful daughter of a Brahman residing in the city of Prathesthan, who became pregnant at an early age by the king of the serpents, and gave birth to a son, whom they named Shalivahan. The boy was brought up with the potters outside the town, the mother and her father having been driven out from the city on account of the girl having become pregnant without the knowledge of a husband. Tradition in the East often makes the mothers of remarkable people conceive in this manner, and people believe it or not according to circumstances. The youth himself, in the present case, soon displayed great military talents as well as extraordinary wisdom, and decided a difficult case, in which a wealthy merchant had buried, under one of the posts of his cot, a quantity of rice husks, under the second some clay, under the third a sheet of paper, and under the fourth a quantity of coals. He had left the two first to his eldest son, the third to his second son, and the fourth to his youngest. For a long time they could not understand what was meant by these legacies, and they wandered far and wide, taking opinions on the subject until at last Shalivahan was consulted. He at once said without any hesitation: "The husks and the clay represent all the grain and other produce of the fields, meadows, orchards, gardens, &c., and these are to go to the eldest son. The sheet of paper represents the bonds, deeds of mortgages, receipt-books, recoveries, and the interest accruing therefrom, and these are assigned to the second son; while the coals represent all the ready cash, gold, silver, and jewels, which are designed for the third." This decision gave great satisfaction, the fame of the youth spread far and wide, and Vickram, hearing about him, was convinced that this was the person who was to bring about his death. He tried, however, to get him to come to his court, but Shalivahan refused, and Vickram marched an army against him, so as to get possession of his person.

To repel the attack, Shalivahan was provided with a miraculous army by his father, the king of the serpents, and with this he put the enemy to flight, and the king Vickram was killed in the fight. Shalivahan then resolved to return home, and with that view collected his forces, and commenced to recross the river, but directly the troops entered the water they at once dissolved, and a voice issuing from the clouds exclaimed, "Victory! Victory! Oh, Shalivahan, be satisfied with the prodigy you have this day been enabled to perform. Henceforth a new era commences, named after yourself, and you will reign supreme in the southern and western provinces beyond the Nerbudda, but the northern part will still remain under the heirs of Vickramaditya, and be governed by his descendants."

The prophecy was eventually fulfilled, and the Shalivahan era began to be computed from the date that he ruled over the countries assigned to him, while Vickram's son succeeded to the throne of his father.

Thus ends an amusing story-book written by an Hindoo for the amusement of his countrymen, and full of wonderful and extraordinary events suited to their lively imagination. The four tales told by the Veytal, or demon, in the shape of the parrot, the shaloouky, the peacock, and the swan, though somewhat verbose, are amusing and interesting. They are too long to be given here, but the book itself might be republished, or a revised edition of it.

CHAPTER VIII.

THE LIFE AND ADVENTURES OF VICKRAMADITYA, RULER OF KALYANA.

ALONG with all the fictions and wonderful stories told in connection with the many Vickrams, it is necessary to give the real history of one of them. Owing to the exertions of the learned Sanscrit scholar, Dr. George Bühler, this is forthcoming, and he has brought to light the history of the life and adventures of Vickram, ruler of Kalyana, composed by the poet Bilhana. A copy of this manuscript, supposed to have been no longer in existence, was found lately in Jesalmir by Dr. Buhler, and the following is chiefly taken from his analysis of the same :—

The work itself may be divided into two parts; the one contains the history of the Chalukyas and their king Vickram; the other gives the personal history of the poet Bilhana himself. As regards the latter, it is only necessary to state that Bilhana's literary career and his wanderings over India seem to have taken place during the latter part of the eleventh century, and that he appears to have finally settled in Kalyana, when Vickram made him his chief Pundit, and where he wrote the king's life.

Vickram himself is supposed to have reigned at Kalyana from 1076 to 1127 A.D. He was the son of the great king Ahavamalla, who, though a mighty conqueror of other kings, was tormented by a great sorrow. He had no son. He therefore resolved, along with his queen, to do penance and propitiate Shiva. Having made over the kingdom to the care of his ministers, they retired to the temple of Shiva. There the royal couple slept on the bare ground, and entirely gave themselves up to devotional practices, and to the service of the temple. The king gathered flowers for the worship of his guardian deity with his own hands, and the queen swept the floor of the temple and smeared it with cowdung. After they had spent some time in this manner, the king, one morning, when engaged in prayer, heard a heavenly voice which announced to him that Shiva, pleased with his faith and penance, was willing to grant him three sons, the second of whom would surpass in valour and in virtues all the princes of the olden time. "Two sons," the voice added, "will be born to thee by virtue of the merit acquired by thy works, but the second will come to thee by my favour alone." The king was much rejoiced; he told his wife the auspicious news, performed the ceremonies required to complete his vow, gave rich presents to the Brahmans, and resumed the duties of his government.

In due course the queen bore a beautiful son, who was called Somesvara. The king, however, was not satisfied. Remembering the predictions of the heavenly voice, he anxiously longed for the birth of his second son. At last he saw the cheek of the queen again become pale. He testified his joy by showering gold on the Brahmans, and by making other thank-offerings. During this second pregnancy the queen had wonderful cravings, which presaged the future greatness of the child she carried. Sometimes she desired to place her feet on the elephants that guard the points of the horizon; sometimes she called upon the nymphs that are the guardian deities of the quarters of the universe to shampoo her feet; and at other times she eyed the swords, as if desirous to drink the water of their steel. Great precautions were taken to ensure the safety of the precious burden. The lying-in chamber was secured by powerful spells and efficacious herbs, and carefully guarded by learned Brahmans. At last, in a most auspicious hour, and under a most favourable conjunction of the planets, the eagerly-desired son was born. Flowers fell from the sky, Indra's drum resounded, and as the gods rejoiced in heaven, so a festive throng, the recitations of the bards, and the songs of the dancers, filled Ahavamalla's palace.

The child's marvellous lustre, which announced its future greatness, induced the king to call him Vickramaditya. He throve, and grew up a strong and handsome boy, the favourite of his father. Early he showed in his plays that he was destined to be a mighty warrior and conqueror. He loved to chase the royal swans, and to tease the lion whelps in their cage. Later he acquired the various alphabets, and the art of using the bow. Sarasvati also, the goddess of poetry and eloquence, kissed his lotus mouth.

Not long after Vickram's birth, a third son was born, and he was called Jayasimha.

When Vickramaditya had grown up to manhood, and had acquired all the sciences, he was anxious for the battle feast. The king Ahavamalla wished to make him "Yuva raja," or heir apparent, and thus designate him as his successor. But Vickram refused the favour, and said that the dignity of "Yuva raja" belonged by right to his elder brother. In this refusal he persisted, even though his father represented to him that both Shiva's word, and the decree of the stars, pronounced him to be destined for the succession. Finding that Vickram was not to be moved, the king raised Someswara, the eldest son, to the rank of Yuva raja. Royal fortune and the love of the father, however, clung to Vickram alone.

After this, with the permission of the king, Vickram set out on a series of warlike expeditions. It is unnecessary to relate his many victories, or the many enemies that he defeated. On his return home, he had come as far as the Krishna, when he suddenly was disquieted by the appearance of unfavourable omens, which announced some great impending misfortune. He stopped his march, and performed on the banks of the river the propitiatory ceremonies intended to avert the threatened evil. While still engaged in these rites a messenger arrived, and announced the sudden illness and death of the king Ahavamalla. The king, said the messenger, had been supremely happy on hearing of his son's success against the Chola, Pandya, and Simhala. In the midst of his rejoicings, he had been attacked by a milignant fever. Finding that all remedies were of no avail, he had resolved to finish his life in the Tungabhadra, the Ganges of the south. With the consent of his ministers he had travelled to the sacred stream, and had died in its waves meditating on Shiva.

On the receipt of this news, Vickram was deeply affected, and loudly manifested his grief. At first, he refused to be comforted, and had to be disarmed lest he should make an attempt on his own life. After a while he recovered, and performed the funeral ceremonies on the banks of the Krishna.

Vickram then returned to Kalyana to console his brother. Somesvara came out to meet him, and the two brothers lived for some time in concord and friendship. After a while, however, Somesvara fell into evil courses. Pride obscured his judgment; he became suspicious, cruel, and avaricious, so that people began to fall away from him. He even tried to do harm to his brother Vickram, who, finding that he was unable to restrain the king from evil, and fearing his life, left Kalyana with all his followers, taking with him also his youngest brother Jayasimha. On learning that his brothers had fled, the king Somesvara sent an army in pursuit of them. Unwilling to make war with his brother, Vickram avoided fighting, but when finally compelled to do so, he destroyed the army like one mouthful, and also defeated other forces which had been sent against him, until these repeated losses forced Somesvara to desist from persecuting his more talented brother.

Vickram, on being left alone, marched towards the Tungabhadra, on whose bank he rested his army for some time. He then commenced another victorious campaign against his enemies, and married a daughter of the king of Chola. After this a series of wars take place, in which at last his brother Someswara takes part against him, and is finally conquered and taken prisoner. Vickram at first wished to restore his captive brother to liberty and to the throne, but Shiva interposed, and angrily ordered Vickram to assume the sovereignty. Then Vickram obeyed the order of the god, and allowed himself to be proclaimed ruler of the Dekhan.

Someswara appears to have been then imprisoned, and his younger brother, Jayasimha, raised to an exalted position of trust. After that Vickram made further expeditions, subdued everybody, and finally returned to his capital of Kalyana.

The king then fell in love, and a long description of the affair is given. As in all Eastern books, first the charms of the woman are given, beginning with her toe nails, and ending with her tresses. The unhappy state of the lover is then represented, and in love, according to Hindoo literature, there are ten changes in the natural state of men which require to be taken into consideration.

1st. When the lover is in a state of mental trouble, and quite at a loss to do anything except to see one particular woman.

2nd. When he finds his mind wandering, as if he were about to lose his senses.

3rd. When he is ever thinking and planning how to woo and win the lady, and cannot get her out of his head.

4th. When he passes restless nights without the refreshment of sleep.

5th. When his looks become haggard, and his body emaciated.

6th. When he feels himself growing shameless, and has no control over his feelings.

7th. When he is prepared to part with his money and spend everything that he has got, and squander away his wealth.

8th. When the state of mental intoxication verges upon madness.

9th. When fainting fits come on.

10th. When he finds himself at the door of death.

In Europe it has been said that spending money is one of the first and crucial tests of love. So long as a man parts freely, he is supposed to love; and when he ceases to part with alacrity, the object is not so dear to him. This may, or may not be true, but among the Hindoos it will be observed that parting does not arrive till the seventh stage, and then only just before the lover is verging upon madness.

But to return to our love-sick king, whose passion grew to such an extent that his limbs wasted away, and pallor overspread his face. On this occasion, however, Kama was propitious, and he went to the court of the Silehara prince, ruling over Karahatee, and wooed and won the daughter, Chandralakha. Their happy life is then described. In the morning they took walks in the garden, and Vickram pointed out to his newly married bride the beauties of the season of spring-time. He placed her in a swing, and swung her with his own hands. Later the whole harem was called out, and the women amused themselves and the king with gathering flowers from the trees and creepers. Then covered with the pollen of the blossoms they went to a tank to bathe, and to sport in the water. Finally, in the evening after enjoying the bright moonlight, and after making a fresh toilet, the whole party sat down to a banquet at which Sura or Madhu, a highly intoxicating liquor, flowed in streams. The women were soon flushed by this drink, and their odd behaviour and fluent speeches served to amuse the king.

At the beginning of the hot season, Vickram returned to Kalyana, and remained there during the summer and rainy season, entirely devoting himself to pleasure; and he also during that time composed a poem describing the breaking of the monsoon.

But after the rains there came news which aroused him from his luxurious repose. It was intimated to him that his younger brother, Jayasimha, was plotting against him and meditating treason; and the informer added, in conclusion, that the prince would shortly advance with hostile intentions against him.

Vickram was greatly distressed by the news,

which opened out the prospect of another fratricidal war. He sent spies to ascertain if the above facts were true, and on their being confirmed he addressed friendly exhortations to his brother, representing to him that as he possessed already regal power in the provinces assigned to him, a rebellion would not benefit him much. His brother would not listen to reason; war became inevitable, and when it did take place, in A.D. 1077, Jayasimha was totally defeated and taken prisoner.

After the victory, Vickram returned to Kalyana, and enjoyed the pleasures of the cold season. These consisted in hunting parties, at which he slew lions and other large game, hunted boars with hounds, and shot deer with arrows.

And then comes the conclusion. After Vickram had subdued all his enemies, his dominions enjoyed peace and prosperity. The elements even showed themselves propitious; neither famine nor pestilence visited his kingdom. In course of time sons were born to him, who resembled him and gladdened his heart. His liberality to the poor of all countries was unbounded. He erected also buildings for pious purposes to commemorate his name. He built a temple; in front of it he dug a splendid tank, and near it he built a city, called Vickramapura, with splendid temples and palaces.

Once more, after a long period of peace, he had to draw his sword. The Chola again became proud and insolent; but Vickram's army marched on Kanchi; a battle was fought; the Chola was defeated and fled, and Kanchi was taken. Vickram amused himself there for some time, and finally returned to his capital.

As a genuine piece of history of the life of an Indian king, some eight hundred years ago, the above work is particularly interesting. It was the period when India was divided into many separate kingdoms, the rulers of which were always fighting with each other. Having no unity among themselves, and utterly failing in combination, they fell easily under the dominion of the Mahommedan power, when it appeared on the scene, and gradually established itself over a good part of India.

CHAPTER IX.

Concluding Remarks.

The preceding chapters will give an idea of the contents of some of the story-books of the Hindoos, and will also give some idea of their character. It will be perceived throughout that the Brahman is the great card, who always plays the most important role, whether as lover, friend, philosopher, or guide. The same power is held by the Brahmans up to the present time, and though, under British rule, they have lost their influence to some extent, they are still by far the most powerful of the many castes in India. Taken as a race, they are clever and astute, and have as good brains as any other race of people in the world. The Brahman women are the best shaped, the handsomest, the cleanest, and the most subtle in Asia.

In some of the stories allusion is made to dancing-girls. Throughout Hindostan they form quite a class of themselves, and are always engaged to perform on festive occasions, such as the thread ceremony, marriage ceremonies, birthdays, and house warmings, &c., &c. Von Orlich in his travels in India says of them:

"These women wear a profusion of jewels, such as rings of gold set with pearls and precious stones in their ears and nose, and around their ankles are massive rings of different kinds of silver. They are dressed in gay garments, which fall in ample folds around them, and a scarf of the finest texture covers their bosom and neck; while their beautiful black hair hangs down in braids over their shoulders. During their dance, which consists partly in a revolving movement, partly in a springing step, they throw the shawl in various graceful forms about the body, and accompany the music with a monotonous song. Their hands and feet are small and delicate, and the contour of the figure and of the countenance extremely elegant, noble and beautiful. They have a very attractive feminine appearance."

Space will not permit of any lengthened details about them, as their castes and habits, and social position differ in various parts of India. Sufficient to state that—

1st. Dancing or nautch girls have existed for centuries and centuries in Hindostan.

2nd. That many of them have been celebrated for great beauty and intelligence, wit and wealth.

3rd. That they are always more carefully educated than other Eastern women. In the story of the ten youths or princes it will be observed how the mother of Kamamanjari explains to the sage Marichi how well she had brought her daughter up, and what care she had taken with her education. The more beautiful and accomplished a singer is, the more likely is she to be successful in her calling.

4th. That they are essential at every native party, festival, or ceremony in India. No European going to that country either as a visitor or on business, will have left it, without hearing at least once the lively air of "Taza be taza."

> "Oh! songstess sweet, begin the lay,
> Ever fresh and ever gay;
> And once again the tale renew,
> Ever old but ever new."

And this brings to mind that among the stories there is another thing sure to be remarked, and that is the power of love over both men and women, and also the effects of love at first sight, which strikes both individuals at one and the same time, and which cannot be denied, though it is so difficult to be accounted for. On the subject of love the Hindoos have a large written literature, and they deal with it more from a physical and material, than from a sentimental point of view, desire and imagination being, in their opinion, the cause of the malady. They divide their women into four classes—viz., the Padmini, or lotus woman; the Chitrini, or art woman; the Shankini, or conch woman; and the Hastini, or elephant woman. And then follows a detailed description of each class.

She in whom the following signs and symptoms appear is called a Padmini. Her face is pleasing as the full moon; her body, well clothed with flesh, is soft as the shiras, or mustard flower; her skin is fine, tender, and fair as the yellow lotus, never dark coloured. Her eyes are bright and beautiful as the orbs of the fawn, well cut, and with reddish corners. Her bosom is hard, full, and high; her neck is shaped as the conch shell, so delicate that the saliva can be seen through it; her nose is straight and lovely, and three folds or wrinkles cross her middle. Her mouth resembles the opening lotus bud, and her perfume is as the lily that has newly burst. She walks with swan-like gait, and her voice is low and musical as the note of the Indian cuckoo; she delights in white raiment, in fine jewels, and in rich dresses. She eats little, sleeps lightly, and being as respectful and religious as she is clever and courteous, she is ever anxious to worship the gods, and to enjoy the conversation of Brahmans. Such, then, is the Padmini, or lotus woman.

The Chitrini is of the middle size, neither short nor tall, with lamp-black hair, thin, round, shell-like neck; tender body; waist lean, girthed as the lion's; hard, full breasts; well-turned thighs, and heavily made below the hips. Her skin is soft, with the perfume of honey. Her eyes roll, and her walk is coquettish like the swing of an elephant, whilst her voice is that of the peacock. She is fond of pleasure and variety; she delights in singing and in every kind of accomplishment, especially the manual; her desires are not strong, and she loves her "pets," parrots, and other birds. Such is the Chitrini, or art woman.

The Shankini is of bilious temperament, her skin being always hot and tawny, or dark yellow-brown; her body is large, her waist thick and her breasts small; her head, hands, and feet are thin and long, and she looks out of the corner of her eyes. Her mouth is always moist. Her voice is hoarse and harsh; her gait is precipitate; she eats with moderation, and she delights in clothes, flowers, and ornaments of red colour. She is subject to fits of passion, which make her head hot and her brain confused. She is of choleric constitution, hard hearted, insolent and vicious, irascible, rude, and ever addicted to finding fault. Such is the Shankini, or conch woman.

The Hastini is short of stature; she has a stout coarse body, and her skin, if fair, is of a dead white; her hair is tawny, her lips are large, and her voice is harsh, choked, and throaty; her gait is slow, and she walks in a slouching manner. Often the toes of one foot are crooked. Her perfume is like the juice which flows in spring from the elephant's temples. She is gluttonous, shameless, and irascible. Such is the Hastini, or elephant woman.

In addition to the above, both men and women are divided into six classes, viz.—

1. The Hare-man,	4. The Deer-woman,
2. The Bull-man,	5. The Mare-woman,
3. The Horse-man,	6. The Elephant-woman,

according to the size of their limbs and bodies. Hindoo authors then proceed to make a series of deductions to prove that the more assimilated the limbs and bodies of the man and woman are with each other, the greater is their chance of agreement and happiness in married life—the worst unions being the hare-man and the elephant-woman, and the deer-woman and the horse-man; the best being the ones placed opposite to each other. It is a new idea for the West, that husbands and wives should quarrel and disagree, because their bodies and limbs are not suited to each other. But as they do often quarrel, and cannot assign any cause or reason for the same, perhaps Hindoo ideas will act as a new light on the subject.

The ages of women are divided into five periods —viz., childhood, say from birth to eleven; girlhood, from eleven to sixteen; young womanhood, from seventeen to thirty; womanhood, from thirty-one to fifty-five; and old womanhood, beyond fifty-five years. In childhood and girlhood they are pleased with small presents, such as flowers, sweetmeats, and fruit. In young womanhood, they must be won by gifts of dresses, jewels, and ornaments; in womanhood, by attention, politeness, kindness, friendship, and love; and in old womanhood, by flattery.

Three temperaments are assigned to women—viz., the Kapha or lymphatic, the Pitta or bilious, and the Vata or nervous. Furthermore, women require to be considered in connexion with the previous state of their existence; the Satwa or disposition inherited from a former life, and which influences their worldly natures.

Among the Hindoos reference is made as often to the former state of existence as to the future one. It is presumed by them that all men and women have lived previously in some shape or form before their appearance here, and that our lives and events in them often hinge on things which have happened in an earlier stage of existence. It is an easy way of accounting for eccentricities in this life that they are due to a previous state, about which we are completely ignorant. There is much the same want of knowledge about our future, and the only thing to be done is to hope for the best.

The Lokayatikas, a sect of free-thinkers, used to argue against the existence of any kind of individuality in a future life, on the grounds of our ignorance of the same in any former existence. Perhaps they thought that the two were bound up together, and must be considered as a whole, and connected with each other.

To return, however, to the Priti, or love-tie connecting men and women; and of this there are four kinds—

1. Naisargiki-priti is that natural affection by which husband and wife cleave to each other like the links of an iron chain. It is a friendship among the good of both sexes.

2. Vishaya-priti is the fondness born in the woman, and increased by means of gifts, such as sweetmeats and delicacies, flowers, perfumery, and preparations of sandal wood, musk, saffron, and so forth. It partakes, therefore, of gluttony, sensuality, and luxury.

3. Sama-priti is also so far sensual, as it has connection with the feelings of both husband and wife.

4. Abhyasaki-priti is the habitual love bred by mutual society; it is shown by walking in fields, gardens, and similar places, by attending together at worship, penances, and self-imposed religious observances, and by frequenting sportive assemblies, plays and dances, where music and similar arts are practised.

Leaving many other details connected with the love of man for woman, and *vice versâ*, there will also be observed among the stories a continual reference to the powers obtained by pilgrimages, religious vows, austerities, and devotions. Any visitor to Benares and other holy places in India will have remarked what a strong hold these have upon the Hindoo mind even of to-day. Religious mendicants, pilgrims, performers of vows, and other wanderers, with or without a religious object in view, are as plentiful there "as leaves in Vallombrosa."

For centuries and centuries the pious Hindoo has regarded Benares as his sacred city, while the broad Ganges has ever been to him the living water, which would wash his sins away. Much has been written against the tenets of the Hindoo faith. It is not, perhaps, so pure to-day as in those ages past, when the early Aryans sang their Vedic hymns, dedicated to things visible and invisible. But still there is as strong a religious feeling throughout Hindostan as throughout Europe, and charity and good works are practised just as much in both countries; and to the student of the various religious sects classed under the main heads of Hindoos and Buddhists, Jews and Christians, Zoroastrians and Mahommedans, the moral maxims of the Vedas will bear an equal comparison with the morals contained in the Tripitika, or three baskets, the Old and New Testaments, the Zenda Vesta, and the Koran.

Another thing that will be noted during a perusal of the stories is the total absence of dates. It is this want which has worried the inquirer into Indian history, archæology, and antiquities generally; and which has compelled him to resort to a vast series of conjectures, which might have been easily cleared up, had proper and reliable dates been forthcoming. For the perfect elucidation of the Hindoo religion, of the many dynasties which have ruled in various parts of Hindostan for centuries and centuries, and for a complete history of early India and of Sanscrit literature, a lot of reliable dates is absolutely necessary. The subject has long attracted the attention of both the scholar and the antiquarian; and, with the aid of inscriptions that have been found both above and below the earth, in the shape of stones, copper-plates, boundary marks, &c., it is hoped that some definite data will eventually be worked out, which may be accepted as a final solution of the question.

In conclusion, the stories will be found to contain an enormous amount of essential matter, which could be worked up into many other forms and shapes. Many books contain some good things, but they are mixed up with such a mass of padding that the gems of the work are lost in their surroundings. In compiling the present work much has been omitted that would be, doubtless, interesting perhaps to the few, but not to the many for whose edification the book has been prepared, and published as cheaply as possible.